JOHN DEWEY

Recollections

Robert Bruce Williams, Ed.D., A.C.S.W.

Graduate Professor of Education and
Social Work Emeritus, Montclair State
College, Upper Montclair, New Jersey

UNIVERSITY
PRESS OF
AMERICA

John Dewey's letters are quoted with the permission of
the Center for Dewey Studies, Southern Illinois
University at Carbondale, ©1981.

Library of Congress Catalog Card Number: 81-40841

TABLE OF CONTENTS

EDITORIAL PREFACE

The present volume is designed primarily as a collection of personal reminiscences about John Dewey. They were obtained in response to an appeal that was mailed to a number of philosophers and educators throughout the United States. It was sent "with the thought that you, as a student, a fellow teacher, or as a friend, may have personal recollections of John Dewey. Your contact with him may have been over a period of time, or it may have been brief, such as attending one of his lectures, or being present at a particular function that involved him in some way." The appeal was given support in the "Author's Queries" of The New York Times Book Review,[1] as well as a reference in an educational journal.[2]

Interest in this writing has been fired from a number of sources. One of these stems from the fact that the author holds something in common with Professor John Dewey: both trace connections with Oil City, Pennsylvania. Immediately following his graduation from the University of Vermont, Dewey taught for two years in the writer's hometown high school. This is discussed in The Peabody Journal.[3]

Another reason is that time does not permit one the indulgence of postponing historical research indefinitely - particularly research that is based upon personal recollections. Important sources of reminiscence about Dewey are frequently passing from the human scene. It was thus reasoned that there must still be a veritable "reservoir of memories" among individuals still living, who have had, in one way or another, some contact with this great educator and philosopher. Hence, unless a deliberate effort is made to capture the still available fragments, the tapestry of human chronicle remains only a partial record. Considerable

---

[1] May 24, 1970, p. 36.
[2] The Journal of the International Association of Pupil Personnel Workers (September, 1970), p. 240.
[3] Robert Bruce Williams, "John Dewey and Oil City," The Peabody Journal 46 (January, 1969), pp. 223-226.

has been written, for example, concerning Dewey's experimental philosophy and its application to such fields as education, psychology, art, and religion. The personal encounter, however, seems important as a vehicle that might well provide some additional insights into the man himself. Such reminiscences are supplemented with a variety of recollections and accolades derived from the literature. Entries are arranged alphabetically. The index lists the names of respondents and authors, in addition to nearly 400 general topics.

Robert Bruce Williams

FOREWORD

John Dewey's distinctiveness lies partly in the fact that he was a great American philosopher. Because he had the insight to perceive that the free society is a _sine_ _qua_ _non_ for freedom of inquiry, of thought, and of action, his distinctiveness lies as well in the fact that he was a philosopher of democratic America. In recognition of his contributions to American political, educational, and social thought, the United States Government has issued a John Dewey memorial postage stamp. He is the only philosopher to have been so honored.

Time has a way of blurring fact with fiction, myth, and legend. It is for this reason that Professor Williams' collection of letters recounting first-hand impressions of Dewey's personality, character, thought, and activities is so timely and refreshing. It is all here--the bitter with the sweet, the chaff with the wheat--and the reader is at liberty to draw his own conclusions. The fact that the impressions are so varied bespeaks the many facets of Dewey, as well as the numerous ways in which his writings have been interpreted.

Included also are excerpts from Dewey's own correspondence--hitherto unpublished. This collection succeeds in "humanizing" Dewey, and in affording the kind of intellectual excitement that Dewey himself so often generated among his listeners and readers. These letters virtually bring Dewey to life again. They offer a perspective on Dewey the philosopher and Dewey the man that to my knowledge is unprecedented.

- Frederick C. Neff
Wayne State University

MONTCLAIR STATE COLLEGE
SCHOOL OF EDUCATION
UPPER MONTCLAIR, NEW JERSEY   07043

May 1, 1970

   This letter is being sent with the thought that you, as a student, a fellow teacher, or as a friend, may have a personal recollection of John Dewey. Your contact with him may have been over a period of time, or it may have been brief, such as attending one of his lectures, or being present at a particular function that involved him in some way. Reminiscences will form part of a volume to be titled, "John Dewey: Recollections."

   Hopefully, responses should be received by me no later than October 1, 1970.

   Your kindness in this matter is very greatly appreciated.

                    Sincerely yours,

                    Robert Bruce Williams, Ed.D., ACSW
                    Associate Professor of Education
                    and Social Work

RBW:oxy

_____

N.B. If you are not able to comply with this request, perhaps you would be kind enough to pass it along to another who could respond in terms of reminiscence.

x

ACKNOWLEDGEMENTS

Sincere thanks are extended to correspondents who have generously contributed to the present volume. Appreciation is also expressed to publishers for permission to use extended quotations (Prometheus Books, <u>Claremont Quarterly</u>, <u>The Derrick</u>, John Wiley and Sons, and <u>Journal of the History of Philosophy</u>. A special debt of gratitude is expressed to Mrs. Elizabeth Bailey who typed the original manuscript with painstaking accuracy.

In addition, I am warmly indebted to Dr. Frederick C. Neff of Wayne State University, whose Foreword is in the tradition of literary excellence.

Thanks are also extended to Dr. Jo Ann Boydston, Project Director for The Center for Dewey Studies, Southern Illinois University, who kindly reviewed the manuscript and, on behalf of The Center for Dewey Studies, gave permission to quote John Dewey's letters.

The supportive interest of Mrs. Martin J. Lauffer is gratefully acknowledged.

Deepest appreciation is extended to my wife Ruth, for her constant encouragement and invaluable assistance in content arrangement.

- Robert Bruce Williams
  Montclair State College
  November 4, 1981

RBW:oxy

Morgan, George W. <u>The Human Predicament: Dissolution
and Wholeness</u>. New York: Dell Publishing Co.,
Inc., 1968.

To understand history is not to reduce the past to concepts and principles dominant in the tiny scope of the
here and now; it is, on the contrary, to widen horizons,
expand and revise present ideas and ideals, and enlarge
oneself by imaginatively experiencing the past. - 177

Adams, George P. and Montague, William Pepperell (eds.).
    <u>Contemporary American Philosophy</u>, Vol. II.
    New York: Russell and Russell, 1962.

Dewey observes,

Upon the whole, the forces that have influenced me have
come from persons and from situations more than from
books - not that I have not, I hope, learned a great
deal from philosophical writings, but that what I have
learned from them has been technical in comparison with
what I have been forced to think upon and about because
of some experience in which I found myself entangled. -
p. 22.

Allport, Gordon. <u>Becoming</u>. New Haven: Yale Universit
        Press, 1955.

Educational practices show its (psychology's) effect,
with teachers and administrators conversing in the idio
of Dewey, Thorndike, Rogers, or psychoanalysis. - 1

Archambault, Reginald D. (ed.). <u>John Dewey on Education</u>:
        <u>Selected Writings</u>. New York: Random House,
        Inc., 1964 - pp. xiii-xxx, author's Intro-
        duction.

.....[Dewey's] early training in Scotch commonsense
philosophy at Vermont, and his introduction to the dyna-
mism and continuity of Hegelianism as a graduate student
at Johns Hopkins were early influences that nourished
his thought.....From William James he learned the principles of the new functional psychology; from Charles
Sanders Peirce the Darwinian framework of challenge,
response, irritation and doubt that would serve as the
basis for his theory of inquiry; from George Herbert
Mead the importance of the new social psychology.

Grinnell College
Grinnell, Iowa
December, 1963

George E. Axtelle
6262 Beadnell Way - Apt. P2
San Diego, California 92117

April 26, 1969

Professor Robert Bruce Williams
Montclair State College
Upper Montclair, NJ   07043

Dear Professor Williams:

I must apologize for my neglect in answering your inquiry regarding Dewey's former students and associates.

You may be interested that the archivist at Southern Illinois University has for the past three or four years been building up what he calls an oral library of Deweyana. He has been conducting interviews and taping them, of everyone who was associated with Dewey. These interviews however are available only on the permission of the interviewee. He has developed quite a library, although people who were associated with Dewey are becoming scarcer each year.

I am sending your letter to Mrs. Jo Ann Boydston, who is now Director of the Dewey Project, in order that she may get a copy of your article. She has brought together the most extensive collection of Deweyana extant. By the way our first two volumes are out. I think you would find them very interesting. You might have your library order them. They are published by the Southern Illinois University Press. Their Titles are: The Early Works of John Dewey, Vol. I and 2. Volume I is entitled Early Essays and Leibnitz New Essays. Volume 2 is his Psychology. It is amazing to see the quality of his writing even in his early twenties. He had published about nine hundred pages of material by the time he was 29.

Sincerely,

George Axtelle

4

George E. Axtelle
6262 Beadnell Way - Apt. P2
San Diego, California 92117

May 22, 1970

Professor Robert Bruce Williams
Montclair State College
Upper Montclair, New Jersey   07043

Dear Professor Williams:

I never met Professor Dewey until I moved to New York City in 1946. However I did not make any effort to meet him personally because I felt that with his advanced years at that time it would be an imposition to impose a new acquaintance upon him.

However Mrs. Kilpatrick had a birthday party for Professor Kilpatrick to which she invited a number of their friends including Mr. Dewey and me. Three things were memorable at that time. First his little adopted son brought a boquet of wild flowers for Professor Kilpatrick and said that when he was a hundred (Professor Kilpatrick) he would send him another boquet by his father. The second was that my son who was interested in photography at the time took a picture of the party which I cherish. Third, Mrs. Kilpatrick placed me next to Mr. Dewey at the table. One thing I remember of our conversation was Mr. Dewey's remark that he always enjoyed having young children about him while he worked at his typewriter.

After that I did make an appointment to meet Mr. Dewey at his apartment. During our conversation I asked him which of his books did he consider his favorite. We discussed several, Experience and Nature, Quest for Certainty, Art as Experience, Logic, and Human Nature and Conduct. He thought that Experience and Nature best set forth his general position, he thought he liked Human Nature and Conduct best. This delighted me because it has always been my favorite. But I have wondered whether that may have been because it was the first of his books with which I became familiar.

5

I need not say that Mr. Dewey was a gentle and modest person, because that is generally known, but I was particularly impressed by them as characterizing him.

Sincerely yours,

George Axtelle

University of New Mexico

Dear Prof. Williams:

I'm afraid I do not have much for you. I met John Dewey
only once, so far as I can recall. While still a graduate student at the University of Michigan, I hitchhiked
to the Eastern Division meetings at Bryn Mawr and Dart-
mouth, during the Christmas holidays of 1932-1933. On
one of these occasions, I arrived at the annual banquet
after all others had been seated, and someone added an
extra chair for me at the end of the table next to
Dewey, who was, until then, the last person on the side.
I do not recall much of the conversation, except that he
very kindly, and considerately inquired about my work
and interests (I had been studying with Roy Wood
Sellars), and treated me very much as a person, while
continuing his conversations with others.

Cordially,

Archie J. Bahm
Professor of Philosophy

THE BARNES FOUNDATION
Merion Station
Montgomery County
Pennsylvania
19066

The Art Department   September 21, 197

Prof. Robert Bruce Williams
Montclair State College
School of Education
Upper Montclair, New Jersey   07043

Dear Prof. Williams:

In response to your letter requesting remembrances of
John Dewey, I am sending you the following five
sketches. My relationship with Dewey was usually
through Dr. Albert C. Barnes rather than by direct
contact, and most of what I have to relate, with the
exception of the last two episodes, in which I have
indicated my presence, were told to me by Dr. Barnes.
The accounts are in the way of anecdotal asides; I do
not know whether they are particularly what you had in
mind, but they do seem to me to indicate something of
Dewey's temperamental and mental processes.

(1)   In the early days of their friendship, Dewey
       mentioned to Dr. Barnes that, in contrast to
       the other arts, music was for him merely a
       physical thing. Dr. Barnes determined to
       teach Dewey to "see" music in terms of its
       embodying the material for experience, and to
       this end he took Dewey to the peanut gallery
       a number of times to hear Stokowski conduct
       the Philadelphia Orchestra. During the inter-
       missions and following the concerts, Dr.
       Barnes drew comparisons for Dewey between
       what happens in music and in paintings until,
       after a few sessions, Dewey acknowledged that
       he had, in fact, come to understand what music
       was about.

(2)   Dewey and Dr. Barnes sometimes travelled to
       Europe together to study in the museums with
       groups of students. On one such occasion
       during a visit to the Prado in Madrid, as Dr.

8

Barnes was talking about the paintings, Dewey stood among the students throwing peanuts up in the air and catching them in his mouth -- much to Dr. Barnes' annoyance. When Dr. Barnes later remonstrated him in a joking way, Dewey insisted that he had heard every word of the talk and challenged Dr. Barnes to put him to the test. Dr. Barnes complied, and Dewey emerged victorious.

(3)   A similar episode occurred on shipboard during an Atlantic crossing. Dewey was an avid reader of detective stories, which he swallowed one after another at an amazing clip. Dr. Barnes banteringly insisted that he must be skipping pages, to which Dewey responded by offering to pick up the story from any place in one of the books that Dr. Barnes might select. Dr. Barnes opened a book to a random page and read the beginning of a sentence aloud, which Dewey then proceeded to complete almost verbatim.

(4)   Dewey's observations on art were sometimes characterized by a remarkable spontaneous insight. On one of his frequent visits to The Barnes Foundation during which Dr. Barnes and I were looking at the collection with him, he stopped in front of a Cezanne, "The Bibemus Quarry," and said with the air of tossing off an incidental remark, "If you were to explode a bomb in the middle of this landscape you would have a Soutine."

(5)   When Dewey was very ill at Bryn Mawr (suburb of Philadelphia) Hospital (where he was being checked up by one of Dr. Barnes' doctor friends) and not expected to recover and Dr. Barnes and I were visiting him, he said in a calm, resigned sort of way, "I have had my piece of pie."

Sincerely,

Violette de Mazia,
Director of Education
    Art Department

Bernstein, Richard J. <u>John Dewey</u>. New York:
          Washington Square Press, 1966 - p. 176.

I do not think that it can be denied that Dewey did have
an optimistic outlook, and that he did believe that the
day would come when intelligence would pervade the democratic community through the medium of education.

Dr. Marguerite Block
Butler Hall, 400 W. 119th Street
New York, NY 10027

June 5, 1970

Dear Mr. Williams,

Here is a story about Professor Dewey which I
heard when I was a graduate student in the Department of
Philosophy. It seems that he gave a lecture or address
somewhere which the students wanted to publish in their
paper, so they had it taken down in shorthand (it was
before the day of tape-recorders). Then they took their
typed transcription to Professor Dewey for his O.K. He
read it and then said, disgustedly, "This is dreadful
stuff - you can't publish it: who wrote it?"

I can sympathize with him, because the same thing
happened to me once, when I spoke at a Swedenborgian
Convention. The things one _says_, seldom sound the same
when you see them in print! It is a good way to deflate
your ego!

Good luck for your book.

Sincerely,

(Dr.) Marguerite Block
Associate in Religion
Columbia University
Retired

P.S. When I was in the Far East in 1958/59 I found that
Professor Dewey's name is highly venerated in Japan and
Thailand especially. Their educational system is really
based on his theories of progressive education. I visited the College of Education in Bangkok and found that
Professor Dewey is considered their patron saint. Interesting, isn't it, when you consider how his reputa-
tion has gone down in America. They were disappointed
to hear that I had never been in one of his courses. He
had retired from teaching before I began my graduate

11

studies. I had done my undergraduate work long before
at Radcliffe, when the only course in Philosophy I took
was with Professor Perry. I was so bored that I dropped
it at midyears! I never dreamed then that I would even
tually get a Ph.D. in Philosophy at Columbia! At Radcliffe I majored in Political Science. One never knows
what the future will bring forth! Life is so unexpect-
ed!

Borrowman, Merle L., "Traditional Values and the Shaping
of American Education," 144-170, in Nelson B.
Henry (Editor). <u>Social Forces Influencing
American Education</u>. Chicago: The University
of Chicago Press, 1961.

.....American industry moved in a direction paralleling
that proposed by Dewey.....the "whole worker" came to be
of concern to management..... - 156

Bourne, Randolph S., "John Dewey's Philosophy," <u>Writin</u>
     of Today: Models of Journalistic Prose.
     Edited by J. W. Cunliffe and Gerhard R. Lomer.
     New York: The Century Company, 1919, p. 175.

     Professor Dewey's thought is inaccessible because
he has always carried his simplicity of manner, his
dread of show or self-advertisement, almost to the poin
of extravagance. In all his psychology there is no
place for the psychology of prestige. His democracy
seems almost to take that extreme form of refusing to
bring one's self or one's ideas to the attention of
others. On the college campus or in the lecture-room h
seems positively to efface himself. The uncertainty of
his silver-gray hair and drooping mustache, of his
voice, of his clothes, suggests that he has almost studied the technique of protective coloration. It will do
you no good to hear him lecture. His sentences, flowing
and exact and lucid when read, you will find strung in
long festoons of obscurity between pauses for the await-
ed right word. The whole business of impressing yourself on other people, of getting yourself over to the
people who want to and ought to have you, has simply
never come into his ultra-democratic mind.

     This incapacity of imagining his own distinction
has put him in the paradoxical situation of a revolu-
tionist with an innate contempt for propaganda. His
philosophy of 'instrumentalism' has an edge on it that
would slash up the habits of thought, the customs and
institutions in which our society has been living for
centuries. He allies himself personally with every
democratic movement, yet will not preach.

14

Bowyer, Carlton H. <u>Philosophical Perspectives for
Education</u>. Glenview, Ill.: Scott, Foresman
and Company, 1970 - p. 3 Introduction.

Fortunately for American education, the educators
who dominated the scene in the early 1900's--men such as
John Dewey (1859-1952), Harold Rugg (1886-1960), and
George S. Counts (1889-   )--were social minded, and
they pioneered the social foundations movement. These
men were the avant garde, the kinds of educators who
have no fear of asking nor of being asked probing questions about the relationship among educational ideals,
practices, and outcomes.

Boydston, Jo Ann, "Three Independent Factors in Morals,"
(Communication presented to the French Philo-
sophical Society by Professor John Dewey of
Columbia University, Translated by Jo Ann
Boydston) Educational Theory, XVI (July, 1966)
197-209.

Mr. Xavier Leon: .....your [Dewey's] philosophy ha
claimed the attention of thinkers in France for quite a
long time and in the meetings of our own Society [The
French Philosophical Society], the question of pragmatism has been discussed on several occasions.

Southern Illinois University
Carbondale, Illinois   62903

Research and Projects Office
Co-operative Research on Dewey Publications

April 28, 1969

Mr. Robert Bruce Williams
Associate Professor of
   Education and Social Work
Montclair State College
Upper Montclair, New Jersey   07043

Dear Professor Williams,

Thank you very much for writing about your article in
the Peabody Journal of Education. I'm looking forward
to reading it and to adding copies of it to our collections here.

George Dykhuizen of the University of Vermont, whose
articles you may know, is engaged in writing a biography. He has written the China-Japan section, and is
well along with the Columbia period. When these are
added to his earlier work, and the whole thing revised,
he will have a book. This is the only full-length work
of its kind I know about.

Our University Archivist, Kenneth Duckett, launched an
oral history project on Dewey a number of years ago. I
believe the kinds of material he developed are similar
to those you would like to do. I'm enclosing a list of
persons interviewed; I believe under the agreement we
have with the interviewees, a number of these can be
studied here at Morris Library.

If there's any further information I can give you,
please let me know. I very much appreciate your interest and assistance.

Sincerely yours,

Jo Ann Boydston
Project Director

JAB/hw
Enclosure

17

(Submitted by Dr. Jo Ann Boydston)

ORAL HISTORY INTERVIEWS

Brand Blanshard

E. A. Burtt

George Counts

Sabino Dewey

James T. Farrell

Horace Friess

James Gutmann

Horace Kallen

Charles A. Madison

Myrtle McGraw

Thomas Munro

Ernest Nagel

Bruce Raup

Louise Romig

Herbert W. Schneider

Harold Taylor

Southern Illinois University
Carbondale, Illinois 62903

Research and Projects Office
Co-operative Research on Dewey Publications

May 14, 1970

Professor Robert Bruce Williams
School of Education
Montclair State College
Upper Montclair, New Jersey 07043

Dear Professor Williams,

I am not able to send you any personal recollections of
John Dewey as I never knew him, but as you suggest I
will pass your note along to another person. As you
know, George Counts is still on our campus and if you
could get a contribution from him, it would seem to me
quite valuable.

Sincerely yours,

Jo Ann Boydston
Project Director

JAB/hw

cc Mr. George Counts

Springfield College
Springfield, Massachusetts   01109

July 16, 197(

Professor Robert B. Williams
Montclair State College
School of Education
Upper Montclair, New Jersey

Dear Professor Williams:

The memo you have circulated about John Dewey
evokes two pleasant memories. One was his generosity in
offering to react to part of the manuscript of my book,
A Philosophic Approach to Communism, later published by
the University of Chicago Press. This was in the early
thirties, when a few American intellectuals, aroused by
the Great Depression, were beginning to take Marxian
theory seriously. Dewey didn't read all of the manuscript; he wrote me that he considered himself too inex-
pert in the subject. His criticisms were insightful
nevertheless, and they did demonstrate that he was con-
cerned about a theory that his own philosophy had not
hitherto considered very much. Later he reviewed the
book quite appreciatively, and I shall always cherish
this review more than any other.

The second memory is of a birthday party in honor
of William H. Kilpatrick in his home arranged by his
wife. Besides Dewey himself, the only guests present
were six or seven young educators in the New York area.
During an affectionate evening of conversation (I still
have a photograph of all of us around a beautifully
lighted birthday cake), Dewey told a hilarious story
that had gone around about Mortimer J. Adler, who had
once been a vocal student of his at Columbia. Adler, we
remember, was early enamored of Thomism and Neo-Thomism
(and still is, I think). But, according to the story,
he was having difficulty in meeting one small rule for
his bachelor's degree: to pass a swimming test as a
physical education requirement. He would go to the pool
often enough, and tip his toes in the water, but apparently could never quite bring himself to jump all the

way in. "And that," said Dewey (I clearly recall his slow, calm way of speaking) "is just the way Adler has always behaved about the Roman Catholic Church!" I am sure Dewey never claimed the story to be true, but surely it was delightful to listen to.

Sincerely,

Theodore Brameld
Visiting Professor of
Urban Life

TB:as

Orville G. Brim
Indian Mountain Road
Lakeville, Conn.   06039

August 30th, 197

Dr. Robert Bruce Williams
Montclair, New Jersey

Dear Dr. Williams,

I have your letter relative to your volume on Dr.
Dewey. I wish I might add to your material but I can
think of nothing that would be helpful. I was often in
Dr. Dewey's class and a student of his writings for all
the years of my teaching. I met him frequently in conference and on social gatherings. The quality that
impressed me most was that, in spite of the many significant problems that occupied his mind, he was always
most willing to listen to any question or thought you
might have, consider it, evaluate it and pass judgment
on it. He never made one feel inferior. I valued my
contact with him highly.

The two men I know who could help you the most, H.
Gordon Hullfish, and Dr. B. H. Bode, both of Ohio State
are dead. Dr. V. T. Thayer, at one time on the Ohio
State Faculty and later head of the Ethical Culture
Schools, is to visit us in a few days. He also knew
Dewey and admired him. I will show him your letter.

With very best wishes for your undertaking, I am,

Sincerely Yours,

(s) Orville G. Brim

Broudy, Harry S., and John R. Palmer. <u>Exemplars of</u>
<u>Teaching Method</u>. Chicago: Rand McNally Co.,
1965.

In 1898 he (Kilpatrick) attended a summer session at the
University of Chicago where he took what he regarded as
a "Disappointing Course" with Dewey. - 148

Far from being disappointed with Dewey's courses at
Columbia, Kilpatrick now became a Dewey disciple at
Teachers College. "The work under Dewey remade my philosophy of life and education," Kilpatrick is quoted as
saying. - 149

Brubacher, John S. <u>Modern Philosophies of Education</u>.
New York: McGraw Hill, 1950, p. 12.

(Re <u>Democracy and Education</u>:) The single best
statement of the democratic ideal in education.....It
had a profound effect on education not only in America
but in the world at large.

Dr. John S. Brubacher
3030 Park Ave., Apt. 8W1
Bridgeport, Conn. 06604

My contact with John Dewey was limited to a class
he taught in Ethics and Education at Teachers College,
Columbia University about 1926-7. The class was disappointing in two ways. First it was a rehash of the
brochure he wrote under that or a similar title.
Second, Dewey's manner was anything but inspiring. I
can still see him entering the dingy classroom late in
the afternoon. Each meeting he would come to the door
and peer in as if uncertain this was the place for him
to lecture. Next he usually searched his rumpled suit
pockets for the slip of paper on which he had the notes
for the day. Having found the crumpled piece of paper
he fixed his eyes on a rear window and launched forth.
Perhaps, as one of his famous students said, it was like
hearing a great man think out loud. It did not strike
me that way but that may have been because I was not a
great student. One of the students, a Mrs. Clapp, read
the term papers so my humble thoughts never even reached
the great man's attention. Certainly there never was
any class discussion for interaction of ideas. Nevertheless, in spite of all this, I am a great admirer of
Dewey's thought.

MONTCLAIR STATE COLLEGE
Upper Montclair, New Jersey 07043

January 21, 197

To: Dr. Robert B. Williams

From: Mrs. Jeannette B. Burbank, Director, Student
       Personnel Resource Center

     John Dewey, generally considered the most illustri
ous alumnus of the University of Vermont, returned to
his alma mater sometime during my undergraduate years
there (1936-39). Many years had passed since his previ
ous visit and his appearance on campus was, therefore,
widely heralded and eagerly anticipated. I cannot recall the occasion which brought him there, but I dis-
tinctly recall that it is the only time I ever saw an
overflow audience in Billings Chapel.

     My first glimpse of Dewey came as he and two or
three faculty members, all in academic garb, entered an
took their places on the platform. I would have judged
him to be about sixty. He was mustached--somewhat unusual in those days--and wore old-fashioned style specta
cles set just slightly below the bridge of his nose. H
was of serious mien, a stern, unsmiling man apparently
completely absorbed in his own thoughts and utterances.

     As a public speaker Dewey left much to be desired;
his voice was of moderate range but not completely dis-
tinct and not well projected. As he spoke he avoided
eye-contact with the audience, either looking down at
his notes or looking out above our heads. Although my
friends and I were seated about mid-center of the hall,
we strained to hear what he was saying.

     The subject of Dewey's lecture eludes me, yet one
moment stands out very vividly in my memory. Looking u
from his notes at one point, and raising his voice almost in anger he remarked that in his extensive travels
throughout this country he had seen NO school employing
instructional methods which he would endorse; and

26

further, having visited practically every teacher training school in the United States, he found not one--"not
even ONE," he reiterated--accurately presenting his
ideas. A murmur rippled through the audience and we
craned our necks to seek out the stony faces of the
faculty. A coarse whisper came from someone a row or
two away, "He just set education back twenty years!"
And in a louder whisper yet, another voice replied,
"FIFTY!"

   Of course, Professor Dewey could not have heard
these remarks, but I am certain he must have been aware
of the response he had engendered in the audience. In
his brief moment of pique and frustration Dewey gave the
impression of a disappointed, disillusioned man--a
rather pathetic figure, I thought, and not at all the
heroic alumnus I had expected to see. This is as I
remember John Dewey.

Butler, J. Donald. <u>Four Philosophies and Their Practic</u>
   <u>in Education and Religion</u>. New York: Harper
   Row, 1951 - p. 371.

     So great has been the acclaim of John Dewey that o
the occasion of his ninetieth birthday, in October, 194
he was honored by a host of men and women who raised th
sum of $90,000 as a birthday gift, $1000 for each year
of his life, which he forthwith invested in benevolent
causes close to his heart. He was also invited back to
his old home in Burlington, Vermont, where he was born
in 1859, the son of the proprietor of a village store,
and was given the rare welcome accorded only to a widel
renowned native son.

(Note: The Center for Dewey Studies adds this comment,
"The goal was to raise $90,000 but the result fell well
below the mark.")

Mrs. W. W. Charters
Pine Croft
Maple City, Michigan 49664

May 15, 1970

Dear Dr. Williams,

My son forwarded your letter to me. Since you are
already in touch with Doctor Wirth, with whom I had a
long interview some time ago, I scarcely know what to
tell you about my several years of study with Dr. John
Dewey, and my other associations with him during the
years till his death.

You may guess that my reminiscences would fill a
book.

I do not remember what I told Dr. Wirth nor what
he used in his book. What I write now may be repeti-
tion.

My first class with Dewey was in the summer of
1901. Dewey had been at the U. of Chicago long enough
to have partially recovered from his Hegelian philosophy (out of which he had written a psychology textbook
which he later wished to disclaim), and was already
much influenced by Wm. James and Pragmatism, and by the
logician Lotze, and also by the social philosophy of
Jane Addams, then the head of Hull House. In fact, one
of my pleasant recollections is of Dr. Dewey's inviting
Jane Addams to his class, his tributes to her, and his
having us students buy Jane Addams "Democracy and
Social Ethics."

I do not know how you plan to use the replies to
your letters. If you wish quotable paragraphs I doubt
if I can supply them. If you wish anecdotes I could
tell numerous ones from the years of 1901-4, and later
when we entertained him in our home in Columbus, Ohio,
where he had been invited by the University Department
of Education (Boyd Bode) for a series of lectures,
which proved of little interest to the graduate students because "it was old stuff" - so completely had
Deweyism been interwoven with all educational teaching.

29

By the time Dewey came to O.S.U. he was so much absorbed with the need for new social action in politics that he had organized in New York what he called "The League for Political Action," and wanted me to organize a "League" in Columbus. (Which I proceeded to do - a separate story, only indirectly connected with Dewey.)

Do you know Dewey's little pamphlet: "The Curriculum and Society," I think it is called? And maybe another, "The Reflex Theory," - small gray books? Both of which reflect his "School and Society"* - all long out of print and probably worth their weight in uranium by now.

I guess I am a sole survivor among those students who took degrees with Dewey in his last years at the University of Chicago. We had a wonderful time with him, and he knew most of us by name!

Cordially,

Jessie A. Charters
(Mrs. W. W.)

*"School and Society" an early book.

Coughlan, Neil. _Young John Dewey_. Chicago: The
        University of Chicago Press, 1973.

[Regarding Dewey's early church experience.]   It _was_
evangelical - a religion of the Bible, not a disguised
rationalism - but it was a quiet, refined, liberal
orthodoxy, more intellectual than experiential. - 5
(Italics in the original.)

George Sylvester Counts
Apartment Community
9500 Route 460
Belleville, Illinois   62223

                                        Aug. 3 - '71

Dear Dr. Williams:

    I knew him [John Dewey] very well personally for
many years.....

                            Sincerely,

                            George S. Counts

MONTCLAIR STATE COLLEGE
Upper Montclair, New Jersey 07043

August 6, 1971

Dear Dr. Counts:

You were so thoughtful to respond to my note. I
trust sincerely that you will soon be feeling strong-
er. I do apologize for what I am sure must be an
imposition. Yet, you were kind enough to say that you
"knew him [Dewey] very well personally for many
years." If I may use this statement, I should be very
grateful to you. Also, I should like to include a
quotation taken from Carlton H. Bowyer, Philosophical
Perspectives for Education, (p. 3):

> Fortunately for American education,
> the educators who dominated the scene in the
> early 1900's--men such as John Dewey (1859-
> 1952), Harold Rugg (1886-1960), and George S.
> Counts (1889-   )--were social minded, and
> they pioneered the social foundations move-
> ment. These men were the avant garde, the
> kinds of educators who have no fear of
> asking nor of being asked probing questions
> about the relationship among educational
> ideals, practices, and outcomes.

If you have any objection to my using such material, please let me know and I shall be pleased to
comply with your request.

Again my sincere good wishes to you personally.

Sincerely yours,

Robert Bruce Williams
Professor of Education
and Social Work

RBW:eb
Enc.

Dr. George S. Counts
Apartment Community
9500 Route 460
Belleville, Illinois 62223

33

```
              Mr. George Sylvester Counts
                 Apartment Community
                  9500 Route 460
              Belleville, Illinois  62223
```

                                        Aug. 16 - '71

Dear Dr. Williams:

     In reply to your letter of the 6th, I am glad to
give you permission to quote anything you wish from my
writings.

     I am enclosing a copy of a letter from John Dewey
sent to Richard Walsh, head of the John Day Co., about
my book <u>The Prospects of American Democracy</u>, published
in 1938.

     Many thanks for your poem!   ["Take Joy"] I like it
very much.

     Very best wishes!

                                   Sincerely,

                                   George S. Counts

THE DERRICK, Centennial Issue (August 14, 1971),
        Section on "Growth in Local Education," p. 15.

Clarence Pelaghi, "John Dewey Started His Career In Oil
City."

In the academic world of education, no name has
become as famous as that of John Dewey.

In the field of philosophy, Dewey is one of the
more important historical figures.

The University of Paris, in conferring a degree
upon him in 1930, described him as "the most profound
and complete expression of American genius."

Dr. W.W. Eshelman, president of the National Education Association, wrote in October 1959: "The indebt-
edness of American schools to John Dewey is without
parallel."

On the cover of Will Durant's book, "The Story of
Philosophy" is this telling statement: "The lives and
opinions of the world's greatest philosophers from
Plato to John Dewey."

A listing of books and majors articles written
about "John Dewey" was recently published in book form
and fills over 300 pages.

In addition to being the subject of many books and
articles, Dewey was a prolific writer himself. In his
lifetime, he published 40 books and 815 articles and
pamphlets.

If piled one on top of the other, his literary
production would tower 12 feet 7 inches high - an output that is not often exceeded.

It is an ironical situation that while the world
has given this man recognition, Oil City almost totally
ignored him.

Dewey was born in 1859 - the same year that Col.
Edwin Drake drilled the world's first commercial oil
well in this Oil Creek area.

And in 1959, when Oil City and the Oil Creek valley were celebrating the centennial of oil, no one locally paid any attention to the John Dewey Centennial that was being observed internationally.

Dr. Robert Williams, a former Oil City resident, set up a national committee in an effort to bring focus on the lack of data on Dewey's sojourn in Oil City.

The New York Times once referred to the period of Dewey's life in Oil City as the "lost years."

Recognition of John Dewey's role in American life was highlighted several years ago with the issuance of a 30-cent John Dewey postage stamp, making him the only Oil City resident to be honored this way.

John Dewey taught two years at the high school on Central Avenue from 1879 to 1881 and lived in a boarding house on the same street.

While his stay here was relatively short, the community played an important role in his life.

Oil City can claim the distinction of providing John Dewey with the spring board to his famous career. A number of "firsts" are associated with his life here:

1. It was in Oil City he had his first professional teaching experience - experience that acquainted him with the archaic methods of teaching that he later resolved so hard to change.

2. It was in Oil City he wrote his first article for publication. It was a piece on philosophy which was published in the Journal of Speculative Philosophy. This initial success in publishing, gave him encouragement to continue writing and helped him make the decision to continue in philosophy.

3. It was in Oil City that Dewey clarified his doubts about religion. He told a friend that it was while reading one night in his room in Oil City that the whole perplexing problem became clear for him.

4. It was his coming to Oil City that severed the umbilical cord from his cloistered life in Burlington, Vt., to the wide world that spread out around him. This was his first step into the pragmatic environment.

36

The boarding house where Dewey lived was located across from the YMCA in the South Side. One of the men staying there at the time was E.V.D. Selden, a young member of the Oil Exchange.

The two became friends and Col. Selden in later years visited Dewey in New York City, after the former high school teacher had become famous.

In recalling his days at the boarding house, Dewey once told a biographer that several oil brokers had urged him to borrow some money and invest it in the town's newest excitement, Standard Oil.

But Dewey did not follow through on the hot tip. Instead, we are told, he borrowed books and used the oil in a lamp for reading.

Col. Selden used to tell an interesting anecdote that occurred in the board house, involving Dewey.

The young teacher did not socialize very much with other boarders. He was described as studious, quite serious, and somewhat bashful. At the common table he was more absorbed with his thoughts than with the food he was eating.

So, when April Fools' Day was coming up, the boarding house operator and other boarders conspired to play a joke on Dewey.

Pancakes were on the menu for that morning and Dewey's got special attention. Instead of the usual ingredients, his were fashioned out of a wooly material and when served looked like the real things.

While the other guests started to eat, they kept their eyes on Dewey as he put the first syrup-soaked piece in his mouth.

Dewey's sudden look of surprise was the signal for a roar of laughter.

Col. Selden explained later that Dewey failed to see the humor in the joke and was not amused in the least.

Dewey also developed a friendship with a pupil in one of his classes, J. Burrell Porterfield, the father of Mrs. Martin J. Lauffer of Oil City RD 2.

Mrs. Lauffer said her father was aware that his teacher was a brilliant man. Porterfield told his family that the young man from Vermont was "too big to stay here."

Porterfield was about 15 at the time and got Dewey's attention because of his excellence in chemistry and physics. Dewey did all he could to get young Porterfield to go on to college.

Unfortunately, the boy's father died and his widowed mother did not have the money to send him on to school. Instead he got a job with the gas company in Oil City where his uncle, Robert Porterfield, was president.

After Dewey left Oil City, Porterfield and Dewey kept in touch with periodic correspondence.

In 1934 Dewey sent Porterfield a copy of his newest book, "A Common Faith."

The book became one of Porterfield's most prized possessions. It is now owned by Mrs. Lauffer.

The Oil City High School has commencement programs for the graduating classes of 1880 and 1881 on which John Dewey's name appears.

Three faculty members are listed: Miss E.A. Kent, principal; Miss Affia F. Wilson, principal of the high school; and John Dewey, assistant.

The graduation exercises for both classes were held in the Opera House. An admission charge of 15 cents was required for the 1880 event; it was dropped to 10 cents in 1881.

There were only six graduating seniors in 1880: Bessie I. Williams, Louisa C. Eichner, Seymout J. Dunn, Charles T. McClintock, Harry H. Culbertson, and William S. Smith.

The group of graduates for 1881 was a little larger and included: Stella F. Duncan, Carrie H. Wright, Effie P. Ross, Ida M. Irvin, Ella McConnell, Tirzah L. Hill, Ida R. Plotts, Jennie A. Berry, Sadie S. Boulton, Alice M. Green, G.B. Swisher, Charles E. Graham, and William R. Duncan.

38

Dewey was paid $40 a month while teaching in Oil City. Only 20 years old that first year, he shared with Miss Wilson the responsibility for teaching 45 students in the four high school grades.

Dewey taught a little of everything including Latin, algebra and natural science from Steele's "Fourteen Weeks."

At 22, Dewey left Oil City in the spring of 1881, taking with him the experience of his baptism in life. Back in Burlington, he arranged for private tutoring with his former philosophy teacher.

After borrowing $500, he set off for Johns Hopkins University in the fall of 1882 - thus launching himself into the mainstream of academic life.

Lake Placid Club Education Foundation
Chartered 1922 by University of State of New York
Melvil Dewey, founder, 1851-1931
Lake Placid Club, Essex Co., NY 12946

June 11, 1970

Dr. Robert B. Williams
School of Education
Montclair State College
Upper Montclair, New Jersey 07043

Dear Dr. Williams,

Your inquiry of June 3 has been passed along to me.

John Dewey, the philosopher, George Dewey, the admiral, Thomas Dewey, the governor, and Melvil Dewey, the librarian, author of the Decimal Classification and founder of Lake Placid Club were all members of the same family, tracing back to Thomas Dewey, the settler, in 1630. They belonged, however, to different branches which separated seven or eight generations back. So far as I know, John Dewey never even visited the Club, altho after I acquired my Ed.D. from Harvard in 1926, my mail got mixed with his occasionally.

Three or four paragraphs on the opening pages of the enclosed reprint of a talk which I gave on the 60th anniversary of the Club present an extremely condensed summary of my father's life work prior to his absorption in the Club. There are at least two published biographies and a third is in prospect in time for the centennial of the American Library Association in 1976.

Cordially yours,

Godfrey Dewey
Vice President

fn/jw

40

Dewey, Godfrey, "Sixty Years of Lake Placid Club, 1895-1955," Reprint of a talk, Agora Auditorium, August 4, 1955.

Objectives of the Foundation

The Foundation charter objectives may be summarized under three catch headings--restorations, schools, and seed sowing. The charter defines the Foundation as--

an educational institution for the purpose
of aiding and restoring to health and
educational efficiency teachers, librarians,
and other educators of moderate means who
have become incapacitated by overwork;
establishing, maintaining and aiding
schools, libraries, or other educational
institutions, especially at Lake Placid,
and instituting, organizing, or fostering
other movements to advance public welfare
through education by means of the Foundation press, conference, forums, addresses,
guided reading and similar agencies;.....

C O P Y

JOHN DEWEY
320 East 72nd Street
New York City

November 4, 1938

Dear Mr. Walsh:

I want to join the many who have expressed warm appreciation of Counts' "PROSPECTS OF AMERICAN DEMOCRACY," and who urged that it receive the attention it so richly merits. Since the publication of this book, any one assessing the prospects for democracy in this country must reckon this book as a great asset on the favorable side if only it is widely read and studied.

As an educator, I should like especially to call the attention of educators to the chapter on the relation of the schools to the future of democracy. I wish I had the power to make this chapter the subject of study in every teachers' meeting throughout the country, including a series of discussions on each one of the eight points he mentions.

It would not only help democracy but will enrich and enliven the teaching in all school subjects.

Sincerely yours,

(Signed) JOHN DEWEY

(Letter from John Dewey to Richard Walsh, head of John Day Co.)

Dewey, John. <u>The Child and the Curriculum</u> and <u>The School and Society</u>. Chicago: The University of Chicago Press, 1956, pp. vi, xi and xii, Introduction by Leonard Carmichael.

Dewey was never a cloistered academician. He did not consider quiet speculation and technical publication to be the only proper role for the modern professional philosopher. He was eager to understand real men and the actual dynamic modern society of which he was a part. He wished to influence the current of events of his times. He was happiest when he saw his ideas in action. And the tonic of his dynamic and pragmatic attitude swept through American, and to some extent world, thinking during Dewey's own lifetime. He was the rare innovator who lived to see his conclusions come to be considered not as revolutionary proposals but as the fixed and established doctrines of a new orthodoxy.

Writing of his personal experiences in Columbia University just prior to 1925, Walter Horton says:

"It was generally understood that there was but one true philosophy, and Dewey was its prophet.....

He wrote from a heart that was full of faith and energy when the pages of our violent and bloody century were still uncut.

Dewey, John. On Experience, Nature, and Freedom.
          Edited, with an Introduction by Richard J.
          Bernstein. New York: The Liberal Arts Press,
          1960 -xxvi Introduction, 13, 15.

Dewey, then, entered the twentieth century with
new and exciting ideas. They were tentatively worked
out and loosely connected, but they were arousing the
imagination and provoking a whole generation of thinkers. As William James prophesied, the discussion of
these ideas was to dominate the American intellectual
scene for the next twenty-five years. (Editorial
comments, xxvi).

.....Upon the whole, the forces that have influenced me have come from persons and from situations
more than from books--not that I have not, I hope,
learned a great deal from philosophical writings, but
that what I have learned from them has been technical
in comparison with what I have been forced to think
upon and about because of some experience in which I
found myself entangled. (Dewey's words quoted by
Bernstein, 13).

.....The third point forms the great exception to
what was said about no very fundamental vital influence
issuing from books; it concerns the influence of
William James. As far as I can discover, one specifi-
able philosophic factor which entered into my thinking
so as to give it a new direction and quality, it is
this one. (Dewey's words quoted by Bernstein, 15).

Dewey, John. <u>Art as Experience</u>. New York: Capricorn
      Books, G.P. Putnams Sons, 1958 - pp. vii-viii,
      Preface.

      In the winter and spring of 1931, I was invited to
give a series of ten lectures at Harvard University.
The subject chosen was the Philosophy of Art; the lectures are the origin of the present volume. The Lec-
tureship was founded in memory of William James and I
esteem it a great honor to have this book associated
even indirectly with his distinguished name. It is a
pleasure, also, to recall, in connection with the lectures, the unvarying kindness and hospitality of my
colleagues in the department of philosophy at Harvard.

      My greatest indebtedness is to Dr. A. C. Barnes.
The chapters have been gone over one by one with him,
and yet what I owe to his comments and suggestions on
this account is but a small measure of my debt. I have
had the benefit of conversations with him through a
period of years, many of which occurred in the presence
of the unrivaled collection of pictures he has assem-
bled. The influence of these conversations, together
with that of his books, has been a chief factor in
shaping my own thinking about the philosophy of esthet-
ics. Whatever is sound in this volume is due more than
I can say to the great educational work carried on in
the Barnes Foundation. That work is of a pioneer quality comparable to the best that has been done in any
field during the present generation, that of science
not excepted. I should be glad to think of this volume
as one phase of the widespread influence the Foundation
is exercising.

Dewey, John, "My Pedagogic Creed," in Jo Ann Boydston (Editor). The Early Works of John Dewey, Volume 5: 1895-1898. Carbondale, Illinois: Southern Illinois University Press, 1972.

I believe that every teacher should realize the dignity of his calling; that he is a social servant set apart.....I believe that in this way the teacher always is the prophet of the true God and the usherer in of the true kingdom of God. - p. 95.

Dewey, Robert E. <u>The Philosophy of John Dewey</u>. The
        Hague: Martinus Nijhoff, 1977.

Dewey was blessed with a long life and the extraordinary
energy to express his views in more than 50 books,
approximately 750 articles, and at least 200 contributions to encyclopedias.....His works have become
classics. - ix

MONTCLAIR STATE COLLEGE
Upper Montclair, New Jersey

Dear Dr. Dykhuizen:

I learn from Jo Ann Boydston that you are coming right
along with your biography on John Dewey. This is
splendid, and I am sure that it will be a significant
contribution.

You will be interested to know that a brief paper of
mine, "John Dewey and Oil City," appears in the
January, 1969 issue of the Peabody Journal of Education.

At the present moment, I am launching inquiry into some
personal recollections of Dewey from former students of
his, fellow teachers, friends, etc. I hope the responses will make it worthwhile.

Again. . .best wishes in your important work!

Very sincerely yours,

Robert Bruce Williams
Associate Professor of
Education and Social Work

RBW:oxy

Dr. George Dykhuizen
University of Vermont
Burlington, Vermont

May thirteenth
1   9   6   9

The University of Vermont
College of Arts and Sciences
Burlington, Vermont 05401

May 26, 1969

Professor Robert B. Williams
Montclair State College
Upper Montclair, New Jersey 07043

Dear Professor Williams:

Thank you for your letter of May 13 which was awaiting me on my return from a conference. I am interested in your article, "John Dewey and Oil City," which appears in the January, 1969 issue of the Peabody Journal of Education, and I hope that you will send me a reprint of it when one becomes available. I have gathered some material on the subject, and will be interested in learning what you have written.

I am glad to learn that you are assembling material relating to personal recollections of Dewey from former associates. Best of luck.

My work on Dewey proceeds slowly because of other duties, but I hope to see it completed in the not too distant future.

Sincerely,

George Dykhuizen
Professor emeritus
of philosophy

Some Personal Recollections of John Dewey

I first saw John Dewey at a meeting of the
American Philosophical Association in New York City in
the early nineteen-thirties. Seated on a couch during
the interval between sessions, he was surrounded by a
group of younger members of the Association plying him
with questions and listening intently to what he had to
say. I was to learn that this was a quite typical
situation at philosophy meetings when Dewey was in
attendance. His modest demeanor, unpretentious manner
and friendly smile dispelled whatever hesitancy one
might have about approaching him.

A few years later, I was to meet Dewey personally.
This was on one of his visits to his native city of
Burlington and to the University of Vermont, his <u>alma
mater</u>. At this and many subsequent meetings, what
deeply impressed me was his warmth, innate courtesy,
and genuine interest in others and the way people of
whatever age or calling immediately felt at home in his
presence.

Dewey did not have a sparkling personality. He
was quiet, unaggressive, and, in a group, was quite
content to sit and listen. When he spoke, it was in a
slow, flat, and rather monotonous voice; large audi-
ences frequently had difficulty keeping their minds
from wandering.

When in Burlington, Dewey liked to reminisce. He
recalled his experience as a youth climbing Mt. Mans-
field or swimming or boating on Lake Champlain. He
told of his summer jobs in the lumber yards on the
shores of Burlington harbor and about the undergraduate
pranks when he was a student at the University of Vermont. Often, on his visits, he would go to the ceme-
tery where his parents, two brothers, and a sister-in-
law as well as many of his childhood friends are
buried. Dewey never forgot his family roots and early
Vermont background.

George Dykhuizen
James Marsh Professor
Emeritus of Philosophy
The University of Vermont

11-1-77

The University of Vermont
Department of Philosophy and Religion
481 Main Street
Burlington, Vermont 05401

February 28, 1972

Professor Robert Bruce Williams
School of Education
Montclair State College
Upper Montclair, New Jersey   07043

Dear Professor Williams:

Thank you very much for your letter of February 18 with its enclosure. The article in The Derrick is very informative and gives me exactly the information I was hoping for. However, a book on Venango County which I got on inter-library loan from the Pennsylvania State Library proved an excellent source of material on Oil City and it was this that I used in the preparation of my manuscript on Dewey.....

You may be interested in knowing that my manuscript on the life and thought of Dewey is finished and has been accepted for publication by the Southern Illinois University Press - probably in the spring of 1973*.

You were thoughtful in thinking of me in connection with The Derrick article and I deeply appreciate it.

With best wishes.

                    Cordially,

                    George Dykhuizen
                    Professor emeritus of Philosophy

GD:ll

*George Dykhuizen, The Life and Mind of John Dewey. Carbondale, Illinois: Southern Illinois University Press, 1973.

Eastman, Max. <u>Great Companions</u>. New York: Farrar,
     Straus and Cudahy, 1942.

     Up in Nova Scotia, where he went in summer, he
still kept the local people in a dither by swimming in
all weathers in the deeps of Solar Lake. Besides surviving this himself, he surprised them one morning by
going out an extra two hundred feet and rescuing, in a
deferential way, a drowning woman. - p. 250

     Dewey never bothered about physical exercise;
brain work, he thought, was just as good, if there was
enough of it. So for recreation he would go on long
automobile rides, and sit in the front seat solving
crossword puzzles and conversing with his companions
..... - p. 269

     He moved out on Long Island, and preserved his
contact with reality by raising eggs and vegetables and
selling them to the neighbors.....His farm was but a
short walk from Walt Whitman's birthplace.....and like
Walt Whitman he loved the companionship of the humble
earth. He loved to identify himself with lowly people.
He was pleased when one day a hurry call came from a
wealthy neighbor for a dozen eggs, and the children
being in school, he himself took the eggs over in a
basket. Going by force of habit to the front door, he
was told brusquely that deliveries were made at the
rear. He trotted obediently around to the back door,
feeling both amused and happy. Some time later, he was
giving a talk to the women's club of the neighborhood,
and his wealthy customer, when he got up to speak,
exclaimed in a loud whisper: "Why, that looks exactly
like our egg man!" - p. 281-282

Edman, Irwin. _John Dewey_. Westport, Connecticut: Greenwood Press, 1955, p. 25.

Dewey all his life retained something of the simplicity of the nineteenth-century world of individuality and fair play, of firsthand respect for firsthand experience that was characteristic of the nineteenth-century Vermonters among whom he grew up.

His [Albert C. Barnes'] book _The Art in Painting_ ....on every page betrays Dewey's influence. _Ibid._, p. 25.

Fairfield, Roy P. (Editor). <u>Humanistic Frontiers in</u>
<u>American Education</u>. Buffalo, NY: Prometheus
Books, 1971.

The roots of the humanist revolution may be traced
back to the revolutionary impact that John Dewey had
upon education. Today it has reached full force, not
only because so many leading intellectuals and educators are committed to the movement for humanistic lib-
eration, but also because, as witnessed by a recent
poll, some two-thirds of American college students,
when asked to identify their basic commitments, responded that they were "humanistic." - xi

It is difficult to envision any humanistic frontier
without John Dewey. One of the intellectual and moral
giants of the twentieth century, he ranks with Bertrand
Russell and Alfred North Whitehead, with Sigmund Freud
and Winston Churchill, as an Everest among the
Himalayas. Even those who disagree with him must admit
that he made a difference in their lives.

Father of progressive education in America, he was
a founder of such liberal and liberating societies as
the American Civil Liberties Union, the National Association for the Advancement of Colored People, and the
American Humanist Association, among dozens of others
with which he was actively involved. He was both ac-
tivist and thinker. Nor did he avoid politics even
when he was abused for his efforts. In 1946, he joined
labor leaders to lay groundwork for a People's Party.
Avowedly antifascist and anticommunist, he spent a
lifetime thinking and writing about the need for developing an "ideal" balance between individual freedom and
institutional forms. His great humanness was felt in
Tokyo and Peking as well as in Moscow and Mexico City,
for his frontier was the whole planet. And despite his
very active involvement in worldly affairs, his published works are estimated to number more than 1000!

One looks back to the future in thinking of Dewey
because so much of what he thought and did was so re-
markably contemporary and relevant. Far from having
failed, as critics of progressive education are so wont
to claim, Dewey's philosophy has never been tried on
any substantial scale. An editorial marking his eight-
ieth birthday sums up his impact:

There are countless school children today
and yesterday whose lives have been influenced
in a constructive way by this one man who
never shouted, and whose formally stated
philosophy often is a stiff dose for more
subtle minds.....One thinks of him as re-
fining into gold the rough ore of our
tumultuous pioneer experience.....He is
yankeeism at its best - shrewd, wise, humane.

The New York Times, May 2, 1952.   114-115

The man lived so compassionate a life. His
modest size and eager soaking up of life's
experiences. His willingness to be "out on
a limb" in his own personal as well as technical principles. It is difficult to approach
his intellectual honesty and accounts of his
life without a response of love and compassion
on one's own part and in return. My listening to him speak to premedical students in a
jammed auditorium at Columbia University,
and the reverence paid him and the record
of his thought at his ninetieth birthday
party and the added aura of worth surround-
ing him as Nehru stopped his round of dip-
lomatic chores to pay homage, recounting
his opportunities to read Dewey while he was
in jail and detailing the effects of Dewey
on his own thought. The greatest power Dewey
had over me as I read his work, being moved
always to extend my own thoughts, develop my
own imagination, asking always, "What does
this mean to me in my work with teachers?"
These are the dominating characteristics:
the measure of the man? How does one take
the measure of a man? As long as controversy
swirls about the work of John Dewey, I will
be pleased. For he provides a matrix of
thought where each of us can freely inquire,
and extend our minding.....as he might say
it.

Otto Krash to Roy Fairfield, February 7, 1970.
- 115

The Green House
Chilmark, Massachusetts 02535

June 27, 1970

Dear Professor Williams,

Your letter of the 17th has just reached me here where
I spend my summers.

My autobiography was published late this spring by Horizon Press in New York, and it is entitled THE WAY OF A
MAN. I don't have a copy with me, but unless I am mis-
taken the Epstein-Dewey episode is reported in it. Alas
the book was published without an index, but I do know
it is full of Epstein anecdotes. If the Dewey bit is
not in it, perhaps I can write it for you this fall if
you have a particular use for it in anything you plan
to publish.

Sincerely,

John K. Feibleman

Tulane University
New Orleans 18, La.

The Green House
Chilmark, Mass. 02535
July 15, 1970

Dear Dr. Williams,

Thanks for yours of the 9th, and for the article on the
"Industrial Arts" which I hope to read before too long.

My respect for Dewey as a philosopher is large, particularly the author of Experience and Nature and the
Logic, but I was never his student. I encountered him
on two occasions. I heard him debate briefly with
Whitehead at some Boston meetings of the American Philosophical Association, though I cannot remember exactly
what year, and I was with Epstein the sculptor when
Ratner brought Dewey for tea because sittings had to be
arranged for a head of Dewey that someone had paid for.
The head, like the one of Einstein, was among the worst
Epstein did.

But on both occasions I thought Dewey, the man, came
off a bad second best. When he was out of a classroom
or study he was out of his depth, a little man at best.
He was intellectually defeated by Whitehead, for he
defended the historical against the logical point of
view, thinking the latter Whitehead's, whereas Whitehead replied, as I remember, that he thought it unnec-
essary to choose, since both coordinates were essential
to any full explanation.

The Epstein encounter was a raucous one. Dewey was ill
at ease in a sculptor's home, particularly one as
superficially disorganized as Epstein's. Epstein, like
most artists, had nothing but contempt for academics.
So he said, with marked sarcasm, "Well, Professor
Dewey, when do you think we should have these sittings?" Dewey got the sarcasm all right, and like most
ill-at-ease people thought to save himself by relaxing
the situation, foolishly said, "Don't call me Professor
Dewey, just Mr. Dewey." But Epstein, who was the
Whistler of his day, shot back, "O well, in London

57

they just call me 'Epstein'", which was perfectly true.
But Dewey was so embarrassed he upset his cup of tea an
seemed completely in rout. I remember thinking that a
true philosopher, one who really was one, ought to be
the equal of any situation that might arise.

If these anecdotes were not in The Way of a Man, they
will be in the next volume, as yet unfinished but in th
works.

Sincerely yours,

James K. Feibleman

Feldman, W. T. The Philosophy of John Dewey. New
        York: Greenwood Press, 1968, p. v.

John Dewey is the dominant figure in American
philosophy today. A host of disciples look upon him
as the great intellectual liberator of our times.

Frankel, Charles, "John Dewey's Legacy," <u>American Scholar</u>.   29:3 (Summer 1960), 313-331.

.....his ideas are in the air and his name echoes.
- 314

.....mind is not a mysterious ghost in the machine
of the body. It is simply one type of physical dispo-
sition and activity. - 325

His most important contribution to the philosophy
of science is undoubtedly his "instrumentalist" theory
of ideas.....The truth of an idea.....is.....its effec-
tiveness in dealing with the particular problem that it
was created to solve. - 326

Gans, Herbert J. _et al._ _On the Making of Americans:_
Essays in Honor of David Riesman. Philadelphia: University of Pennsylvania Press,
1979.

Dewey.....attempts to replace the dark solitude of
private, individualistic conceptions of morality with a
sunlit, public set of standards. Dewey wanted to replace the inner torment of Emersonian subjectivity with
a social, communal, and - in Dewey's reckoning - more
objective set of standards of judgment, to destroy with
his ethical theories the notion that morality was mainly an affair of motives, inner responses to abstract
principle. He hated.....introspective focus on inner
feelings. He hated it when his mother asked him if he
was right with Jesus.....Dewey wanted ethics that focused on what really mattered: action and its visible
consequences. He rejected both the utilitarian calcu-
lating machine and the old appeal to a guilty conscience because they denied the possibility of a common
moral world. He wanted an ideal of character that
would change in response to life, that took a conscious, experimental attitude towards experience. This
is why his ethics were supremely social and communal. -
p. 13

The University of West Florida
Pensacola, Florida 32504

May 31, 1970

Mr. Robert Bruce Williams
Montclair State College
Upper Montclair, New Jersey 07043

Dear Mr. Williams:

Noting your inquiry in the New York Times, I am happy to contribute what I can to your book on John Dewey.

In the fall of 1926, I was a member of the last course Dr. Dewey taught at Columbia: Introduction to Ethics. His manner of lecturing was pedestrian though occasionally he spoke with great earnestness. After class one day I asked him whether he would discuss with us the influence which discoveries in biology might have on ethical concepts. He replied it was an interesting subject, but he did not get around to examining the matter in class.

I saw Dr. Dewey again in Cleveland at a meeting set up by our local chapter of the American Federation of Teachers. He made some remarks to the effect that he supported the aims of the teachers' union. Mrs. Gebauer shook hands with him later. He was quite unassuming in his cordial greeting. My wife suggested that she was an exception to most in the group which was made up of teachers. "I'm just a mother," she said. "Just a mother?" said Dr. Dewey. "Mothers are the first and the greatest teachers."

Sincerely yours,

Emanuel L. Gebauer

May 25, 1970
600-22 Baychester Avenue
Bronx, NY   10475

Robert Bruce Williams
Montclair State College
Upper Montclair, NJ   07043

Dear Mr. Williams,

In your "Authors" Queries in the New York Times Book
Review of May 24, you stated that you "would appreciate
hearing from any friends, former students of his (John
Dewey) and fellow teachers."

I don't exactly fit into any of these categories. I
never attended a university due to disability and fi-
nancial considerations. However, I began a correspondence with John Dewey when I was 18 years old. The
correspondence dealt with the deeper aspects of Dewey's
philosophy. I have the letters from Dewey, although I
lost or misplaced my letters to him. There was one
letter which I believe to be of great import, since in
it Dewey contrasts his philosophy with that of Bergson
and in which he points out quite fundamentally the
distinction between Bergson's intuitive approach to
living and mental realities and Dewey's approach. In
this respect, Bergson was contrasting living and mental
realities to the scientific and logical approach to the
physical world. Dewey emphasized in his letter that
conceptual structures were necessary in both domains.

In February, 1935, when Dewey was 76 years old and I
was 21 years old, he invited me to his office in Philosophy Hall at Columbia University. It was the first
time that I was inside any university. I recall waiting in the corridor outside Dewey's office where there
were other offices with the names of other philosophers
at Columbia whom I had studied, such as Irwin Edman and
Herbert W. Schneider.

Finally, when Dewey arrived, I recall that I was impressed with his vigorous stride as he walked into the
corridor. We entered his office which was extremely
small. There was a very old roll-type desk next to the

only window in the room. It was when Dewey sat down
that he seemed to sag. As I recall, he had a large
head and bushy hair. He was the kind of man who was
simple, gentle, and unhurried in his manner and I felt
completely at ease with him. He gave me his undivided
attention for about an hour. He told me that he was
deaf in his left ear and that I would have to talk
loud. He told me that he was retired and that he had
lost touch with the active teaching profession. Since
the purpose of our meeting was to try to assist me with
reference to a possible career in philosophy, he then
and there wrote a letter of introduction for me to
Sydney Hook, who was a former student of his. Hook was
and still is, I believe, Chairman of the Department of
Philosophy at Washington Square College, New York
University. Unfortunately, I had a recurrent attack of
illness and I never used the letter (I still have it in
my possession).

The meeting with Dewey left a lasting impression and I
remember it vividly to this day.

If there is any way that I may be of assistance to you
please write to me.

                                    Very truly yours,

                              Murray Gishman

Hamilton, Walter H. "Our Man-Made Natural Resources,"
    Resources for Building America. Progressive
    Education Booklet No. 15. Columbus, Ohio:
    American Education Press, Inc., 1939, pp. 58-
    63.

John Dewey "brings to us not truth and peace, but un-
rest and challenge."

Paul R. Hanna
737 Frenchman's Road
Stanford, California   94305

June 9, 1970

Mr. Robert Bruce Williams
Associate Professor of Education
   and Social Work
School of Education
Montclair State College
Upper Montclair, New Jersey   07043

Dear Mr. Williams:

You asked for some personal recollections on John
Dewey. I have written a very short response which I
hope will be found useful.

Cordially yours,

Paul R. Hanna

PRH:cd
Enclosure

Paul R. Hanna
Stanford University

June 6, 1970

My recollections of John Dewey are vivid ones.
His small seminars which I attended in the mid 1920's
were as stimulating intellectual exercises as any I
have ever undergone. His mannerisms in small seminar
groups were highly stimulating and contrasted sharply
with his seemingly "deadpan" delivery of a lecture to a
large audience.

I recall many a philosophical discussion with Mr.
Dewey as several of us would gather around him at the
luncheon table at the Columbia University Faculty Club.
In his quiet manner, in between pipe puffs, he would
ask penetrating questions or make comments that shed
light on a problem of the day. His style indicated a
reserve, even a shyness, but we younger men cherished
the opportunity to participate in discussions in which
he would lead us out intellectually.

My greatest debt to Mr. Dewey, however, developed
in later years as I read his entire works and saw how
improperly he had been interpreted by some of his admirers.

Dewey never advocated a child-centered schooling
at the expense of society's stake in education. For
every paper or volume that Dewey wrote on the "child,"
he balanced the score by publishing one on the responsibility of the school to perpetuate and improve the
society. Dewey was not in sympathy with the extreme
permissiveness and lack of curriculum design that became the benchmarks of the progressive schools of the
second quarter of this century. In fact Dewey spoke
out against these misinterpretations of his philosophy
in the keynote address entitled "The Science of Progressive Education" at an early national meeting of the
Progressive Education Association. He even went so far
as to suggest that he could no longer serve as Honorary
President of the PEA if that organization continued to
stress child permissiveness to the neglect of society
and child responsibility. John Childs wrote a volume,
Education and Morals, in which he made Dewey's balanced

67

position in curriculum very clear. It is unfortunate that more of Dewey's students and admirers did not read Dewey's entire output; to have understood his balanced treatment of curriculum and instruction would have avoided much confusion during the last half century.

Georgia Harkness
1377 Via Zurita
Claremont, Calif. 91711

May 18, 1970

Dr. Robert B. Williams,
Montclair State College,
Upper Montclair, NY

Dear Dr. Williams:

I never had any direct contact with John Dewey. I
heard him read one of the Carus lectures and speak on
one or two other occasions, but did not know him personally. His oral presentation, I must say, seemed
rather dull in comparison with the far-reaching influence of his thought.

A friend of mine, the late Richard Edwards who used to
be the Director of the Cornell University United Religious Work, knew him well and told me an interesting
item which I cannot corroborate personally but you may
wish to look into it. He said that when the Deweys'
little boy died, aged twelve or thereabouts, he would
have no funeral service but asked Jane Addams to speak
and she did so from the theme, "What is excellent is
permanent."

When the first Mrs. Dewey died, he asked Dick Edwards
to conduct the service, and suggested that he use the
Shepherd Psalm, the Beatitudes, and the Lord's Prayer.
At one time I wrote to Corliss Lamont to ask if he
thought this indicated any lingering theism. He replied that he thought more likely it was done out of
respect for Mrs. Dewey.

Many thanks for the good word about the book of mine
that you used in college. It stayed in print from 1929
to 1962 or 1963, which is quite a lifetime for that
kind of book.

Sincerely yours,

Georgia Harkness

69

Holmes, Brian, "The Reflective Man: Dewey," in Nash, Paul, Kazamias, Andreas M., and Perkinson, Henry J. (Editors), <u>The Educated Man: Studie in the History of Educational Thought</u>. New York: John Wiley & Sons, Inc., 1965 - p. 305

Any Englishman who has the temerity to write about John Dewey--a famous American institution--should offer an explanation.....his writings can provide for the European a rationale for American education--a pattern of assumptions and beliefs against which it is possible to make sense of a highly complex system, and what goes on within it. In particular, <u>How We Think</u> seems to offer in a single volume as useful a picture of American educational assumptions as Plato's <u>Republic</u> provides for European education. No better example of this assertion can be found than the title of a recent book by H. Gordon Hullfish and Philip G. Smith--<u>Reflective Thinking: the Method of Education</u>.

I mention this book for another reason too. It enables me to acknowledge the debt I owe to the late Gordon Hullfish personally and to the writings of Dewey and Boyd H. Bode and other progressive educators in the evolution of my thinking about education.

Hook, Sidney (ed.). In Defense of Academic Freedom.
        New York: The Bobbs-Merrill Company, Inc.,
        1971 - p. 11.

I want to stay young, at least in spirit, and I learned
from my teacher, John Dewey, whom I observed closely
for the last twenty-five years of his life, what the
secret of staying young is and that is not to reminisce
about the past. Actually, I never heard John Dewey
reminisce until he was in his nineties, and that was as
a reluctant response to my deliberate prodding in order
to extract biographical data from him.

Itzkoff, Seymour W. <u>Cultural Pluralism and American</u>
    <u>Education</u>. Scranton, PA: International
    Textbook Company, 1969 - pp. 35-36.

.....Dewey's views constitute one of the most importan
philosophical contributions to the definition of the
democratic life in terms of its sources in basic conceptions of man, nature, and experience.....Dewey was
perhaps the most typically American of all philosophers. The New England small-town democracy was certainly important in giving him that perennial optimistic expectancy concerning the efficacy of human intelligence and the sense of possibility that American
democracy contained.

    In 1890 a copy of William James' <u>Principles of</u>
<u>Psychology</u> came into Dewey's hands. The arguments of
this philosopher-psychologist concerning the nature of
human behavior and its biological causes were extremely
persuasive.[1]

[1]Gail Kennedy, "John Dewey," in Max Fisch (ed.),
<u>Classic American Philosophers</u> (New York: Appleton-
Century-Crofts, 1951), p. 332.

Alvin Johnson
200 North Broadway
Nyack, New York 10960

May 29, 1970

Dear Professor Williams:

I'm sending you an account of my relations with John Dewey.

Have you contacted Professor Horace Kallen, at the New School, a favorite disciple of John Dewey?

Sincerely,

Alvin Johnson

Alvin Johnson
200 North Broadway
Nyack, New York 10960

May 29, 1970

John Dewey came into my life when I was an instructor in economics. Dewey was an associate professor of education.   He was seven years older than I,
but that meant nothing to me. My earliest male compan-
ion was my good father, nearly fifty years older, but
one of the old who are forever young.

I married Edith Henry, my sweetheart at the University of Nebraska. She was a very talented Greek
scholar as well as a philosopher, and wrote for her
doctor's dissertation a little book, <u>The Argument of
Aristotle's Metaphysics</u>. We had the book printed and I
gave a copy to John Dewey, who told me that now for the
first time he really understood Aristotle.

Most American philosophy departments had been
taken over by Neo-Hegelianism. This was not true of
Columbia, which still had an open mind. The Neo-
Hegelians felt that all the substantial values of philosophy were drawn from Neo-Hegelianism and to question
them was almost impious. Some years later, when I was
professor of economics at Cornell, a graduate student
of philosophy with a minor in economics brought the
curses of the philosophy department down on his head by
questioning the values of Neo-Hegelianism. The two
professors of philosophy, Creighton and Tillich, decid-
ed that this impious student should be driven out of
academic life. As I took him over into economics the
two philosophers cut me out of their books and never
spoke to me again.

Somehow John Dewey's name and mine became associated over the years. A student who had heard an address by Dewey would ask me to interpret it. Dewey
told me of similar efforts to understand my position.

In one case this confusion was very useful to me.
When Hitler came to power I began bringing over professors from Germany. The German government ordered the
consul to find out what kind of man Alvin Johnson was

74

and what he meant by taking over those scholars. The
consul reported that Alvin Johnson was closely associated with John Dewey. We were both lovers of peace and
friends of the real Germany. It should be a rule of
the German government to grant any request I made for
the exit of German scholars. And in fact that rule
held until the Second World War came on. I had brought
hundreds of scholars out of the claws of Hitler.

There were years when Dewey and I did not see each
other. Once he invited me to come and have lunch with
him and meet his second wife, Roberta. I found them in
a very pleasant apartment. Roberta was moving around
among eight children, four boys and four girls; whom
she was giving the training in humanity John approved.
One was from a very poor household and had come in old
and rather ragged clothes. Roberta had called on the
other children to give from their allowances what would
supply the poor boy with the kind of clothes they wore.
This community undertaking had pulled the children into
a democratic unity.

Roberta was a very pretty little person with the
sweetest face I had ever seen.

"You wouldn't think of Roberta as a capitalist,"
Dewey said, with characteristic gentle humor. "But she
holds a large interest in Pittsburgh Glass. One of
these days the noisy boys who are breaking windows will
begin to cry that they are making money for Roberta
Dewey, and feel that they ought to leave the windows
alone."

In our discussions we touched on the various
schools that had developed in the country known as
Dewey schools. Dewey was sympathetic with the motives
of the schools but felt that they did not really appreciate life. He was continually finding philosophical
implications in the changing patterns of everyday living.

"There is a horrible idea nowadays that old people
should be housed together in groups. Old people need
young people to make life worth while. And young
people need old people. Nowadays parents are too much
occupied with their professional or social life and
their children are turned over to servants. They get
no real sense of lifelong life.

"If I see a man or woman really at home in the world I think he has probably had learning with a good grandfather or grandmother. I think you, Alvin, must have had a good grandfather."

"My grandfathers both died before I could recognize them," I said. "But my father was old enough to be my grandfather and introduced me to the life of animal and plants on the farm. I had a sweet grandmother who introduced me to life in Denmark."

"Now we have time enough," Dewey said, "let us get a little drink and see if we can make anything of Bradley and Bosanquet, and their brand of Neo-Hegelianism." He fixed up two spacious gin cocktails.

"I give it up," Dewey said. "Any cross between philosophy and religion is an infertile cross. Philosophy requires you to think, religion requires you to believe. They may be all right in their place but they need to be kept apart."

I was a rather frequent visitor of John and Roberta. Their happiness was so inspiring for one whose years were soon to turn to the shady side.

Their happiness was not to last. Our good friends, the Bacons, invited the Deweys to go with them to Hawaii. On the way John developed a condition requiring a serious operation. I do not know whether the Hawaiian surgeons were of the most skillful. Anyway, the operation left a wound that would not heal. When John Dewey got back to New York his days were numbered.

His spirit stood up bravely. The last time I saw him he said, he would be waiting at heaven's gate for Roberta. The gate would not be in some Palestine sky, but wherever a man's heart is.

I did not see much of Roberta after John's death. My health was not good, and I remained pretty consistently in my own home. But I got a glimpse of her at my ninety-fifth birthday celebration, and we promised to meet in June. But only a few weeks ago Roberta died.

76

Johnson, A.H. The Wit and Wisdom of John Dewey. New
         York: Greenwood Press, 1949.

     From Columbia, John Dewey went out through the
world, to China, Japan, Russia, Turkey, Mexico, South
Africa. In all these projects he demonstrated, unfail-
ingly, the power of ideals which have a natural basis
in the needs of men. Everywhere he strengthened the
cause of true democracy. - p. 8

     Absence of pretentiousness, and tremendous depth
and power of mind, are essential characteristics of
John Dewey. - p. 39

33 Lexington Avenue
Cambridge, Mass.

September 1, 1970

Dear Professor Williams:

I did not realize that I had let so much time go by
before answering your letter (which I took with me on
my vacation in France). Very likely anything I can
send you now will arrive too late to be useful. Nevertheless, I will jot down a few of the thoughts that
have occurred to me since I began refreshing my memory
of Dewey.

I can confirm what you say about his pleasure in having
children around him. He was charming with them - a
little too permissive according to my more austere
views on bringing up children, but they were certainly
devoted to him. I remember one evening when the two of
them with a minimum of supervision made the cocktails -
"Dewey Specials" - and did a very good job indeed - a
credit to their father's educational principles.

I can also confirm what you say about his capacity for
joy and genuine happiness. Being at the Dewey's was
always a joyous experience. He gave you the feeling
that what you had to say was interesting to him and
that he enjoyed listening as well as talking. So you
went away pleased with yourself as well as with him.

The only time I got into any kind of argument with him
was over the "look-say" method of teaching reading,
which I considered one of the great disasters of American education. I was shocked when Dewey defended it
with what seemed to me unsound reasoning.

Dewey did not think much of contemporary psychology.
(He told me that Adelbert Ames was the only one at that
time, c. 1949, who was making an important contribution
to psychology as a science.) One day I found him with
a copy of Psychological Review in his hands. He threw
it down as I came in and exclaimed, "I despair of psy-
chologists!" On my asking why, he said, "They have no
understanding of what science is. They think it has to
do with measuring and counting." He pointed to the
plastered wall, which had a number of cracks on it, and
said, "If I measured those lines and calculated their
slopes and published the results, that wouldn't be
science but some psychologist would think it was."

Dewey felt badly that psychology was not living up to
its early promise. He had been very pleased when for
the 50th anniversary of the Psychological Review his
article on "The Reflex Arc," was voted the most important contribution to psychology made in that journal.

Most of my conversations with Dewey were about the
"Alexander Technique." It had been in a large part
Dewey's advice that had made me decide to take
Alexander's training course for teachers. He was very
helpful later on in clarifying for me some of the key
concepts in the technique - "inhibition," for example,
and the difference between "thinking" and "feeling."
Dewey grasped the full implications of Alexander's
discovery - that if you can change the way organism
responds to stimuli, you will change its functioning on
all levels, mental and moral as well as physical. The
most important effect of the Alexander training on
himself, he told me, was the increased flexibility in
his thinking - the ability to reexamine a philosophical
position and change it if necessary. None of Dewey's
disciples seems to have grasped the significance of the
association with Alexander. The reason for this fail-
ure has always perplexed me. Someday I plan to write
an article on the subject.

I hope that some of this may be of use to you and that
it has not arrived too late.

Sincerely,

Frank P. Jones

Frank Pierce Jones
33 Lexington Avenue
Cambridge, Massachusetts 02138

May 31, 1970

Dear Mr. Williams,

Mrs. David Riesman wrote me that she had seen a notice of yours in the <u>N.Y. Times</u> asking for information about John Dewey. If I knew what sort of book you are planning to write I might be able to supply some material that would be of interest. I wrote to Dewey in 1941 asking his advice about taking the training course for teachers of the Alexander Technique. He replied urging me to do so. I continued correspondence, and after I had begun teaching the technique myself I had a number of conversations with Dewey and dined several times with him and his wife in their New York apartment. His letters to me are in the Wessell Library at Tufts (see enclosure). In addition I have a fairly vivid impression of our meetings and can remember a little of the conversations I had with him.

I am a professor of Classics (Emeritus) and Research Associate in Psychology at Tufts University.

Sincerely yours,

Frank P. Jones

Jones, Frank P.   "Letters from John Dewey in the
          Wessell Library, Tufts University,"
          <u>Educational Theory</u>, 17, (January 1967),
          pp. 92-93.

My collection of 15 letters and cards from John
Dewey has been deposited in the Wessell Library at
Tufts University, with the right of publication re-
served.

Sabian Publishing Society
2324 Norman Road
Stanwood, Washington 98292

    My first contact with John Dewey was indirect,
when I attended the University High School in Chicago,
1905-8 or about a year after he went to Columbia University. In afterview I could realize that it was his
surviving impact that in particular significance enabled me to find myself intellectually, even if I had
no immediate opportunity to capitalize on it.

    My contact with him in the flesh was in New York
City at Teachers College at Columbua in 1938, when I
was working on my doctorate and at that time was pre-
paring a thesis on his early ideas. I remember most
vividly when as president of the Philosophy of Education Club I was master of ceremonies for the occasion
when I had persuaded him to be the speaker at our
dinner and witnessed the attempt of a very brilliant
fellow candidate for the doctor's degree to maneuver
our venerable guest into a substantiation of some
wholly metaphysical strictures distilled from the volu-
minous Dewey writings, and noted how adroitly the
author then entering his eighties was still able to
deal as he always had been with an essentially hypo-
thetical assumption.

                                Marc Edmund Jones

                    Cold Spring Harbor
              Long Island, New York 11724

                                    June 7, 1971

Dear Mr. Williams:

        If you have not yet been advised, Mr. John Dewey
has a son: Sabino Dewey living in Huntington, L.I.

                            Sincerely,

                            (Mrs.) S. Kamen

George Kaufmann
Attorney At Law

Suite 800, Federal Bar Building West
1819 H Street, Northwest
Washington, D.C.   20006

June 5, 1970

Mr. Robert Bruce Williams
Montclair State College
Upper Montclair, New Jersey   07043

Dear Mr. Williams:

This is in reference to your inquiry in the <u>New York Times Book Review</u> regarding John Dewey. My late father, Felix Kaufmann, conducted a protracted correspondence with Dewey up to the time of my father's death in December 1949. It is my understanding that this correspondence dealt mainly with epistemological problems arising out of my father's study and critique of Dewey's Logic. It is not clear from your necessarily brief notice in the <u>New York Times</u> to what extent you are interested in correspondence covering technical subjects rather than more personal details. If the correspondence is of interest to you, please call me.

Sincerely yours,

George Kaufmann

Wayne State University
Detroit, Michigan

July 16, 1963

The following are some comments concerning Dewey, made
by Distinguished Professor Earl C. Kelley (in a conversation with the Editor):

"Dewey was pretty sick in Arizona and called for me to
come down. I went, and stayed with him a few days. I
couldn't take notes, because it broke the line of
thought; so I came away without any notes. He got
better and I came home."

"He gave me the key to his Fifth Avenue (New York)
apartment, for us to use, but his illness at that time
interfered so we never got a chance to use the apartment."

                    1158 Fifth Avenue
              New York 29, New York

                              September 12, 1947

Dear Dr. [Earl J.] Kelley:

I mailed the enclosed to you from Hubbards, N.S.
August 29th only two or three days after I received
the proof.....By a bad case of absent-mindedness I
addressed the letter to you at Detroit University. I
am very sorry for my carelessness and hope the delay
has not seriously inconvenienced you. You must have
thought it strange indeed not hearing from me. Unfortunately being sorry doesn't help.

                         Sincerely yours,

                         John Dewey

January 1, 1950

Dear Earl Kelley:

I am glad to place on public record the statement
[on].....the workshop. It supplies the missing and much
needed factor in development of the theory of progressive education. For it applies to the <u>training of</u>
<u>teachers</u> the principles that have been set forth as
applicable to and in the education of those under instruction.

Yours sincerely and with the best wishes of the season.

                              Yours,

                              John Dewey

I shall be leaving in a week or so on a trip to
Honolulu.

504 South Street
Key West, Florida

April 10, 1950

Dear Earl Kelley:

What you say about philosophy is exactly the view I
take. Philosophy has been discredited as far as it has
claimed to be itself a science - to say nothing of
being the "supreme science" - I think the Greek "love
of wisdom" didn't mean of "knowledge" - wisdom is judgment about the uses to which knowledge should be put -
Its a "practical" or moral term and "love" "philo" is
emotive - practical philosophy today is largely in
academic doldrums - its "professors" rarely make even
an attempt to use it in its application to life's
issues to say nothing of developing it so it can and
will apply.....Could you point out to me where Ames-
Cantril have held there is a ready made common world
.....certainly the transactional pt. of view holds
there isn't one save as it is made - a human job.

Yours,

John Dewey

```
                    R.D. #1
                  New Alexander
                  Pennsylvania




                                        August 3, 1950



Dear Earl [J. Kelley]:

Elevation about 1000 feet - cool nights lovely
country - trees, hills and valleys.

                                        Yours,



                                        John D.
```

New Alexandria
Pennsylvania

August 4, 1950

Dear Earl [J. Kelley]:

.....I think the article of Fries [Horace Fries of
University of Wisconsin] in the July number of <u>Philo-
sophy of Science</u> stands out like a lighthouse in sandy
shoals.....The Princeton men seem to think that there
is a <u>ready-made</u>, ready at hand <u>social</u> materia <u>which</u> is
ex-officio standard and waiting as the brackets to
receive and hold the Ames conclusions.....Your "sta-
tistical" man gives the proper title to the human
being who is neither <u>biological</u> nor <u>anthropological</u> in
any accultural sense.

Yours with best wishes,

John Dewey

                    1158 Fifth Avenue
                New York 29, New York

                                September 16, 1950

Dear Earl [J. Kelley]:

.....I don't recall whether I happened to write you
about the pleasure I had in an etymological discovery -
namely that "attitude" is derived from aptitude. Unfortunately it is double-barrelled fact. It testifies
not only to the truth of what you say about assumptions
as for sight memory and value judgments but also about
their tendency to get stiffened, fossilized.

The best to you and your partner.

                            Yours,

                            John Dewey

                    1158 Fifth Avenue
                  New York 29, New York

                                        November 9, 1950

Dear Earl [J. Kelley]:

.....You've done a job that needed doing (referring to
the book, <u>Education for What is Real</u>, which contains a
forward by John Dewey) and done it well.

                              John Dewey

1158 Fifth Avenue
New York 29, NY

December 1, 1950

Dear Earl [J. Kelley]:

.....I get pretty discouraged at the turn philosophers
are taking - It is you and a number of others of the
younger men <u>who keep</u> up my courage and resolution to go
on so the more of your own (mss.) you send me the better off I am. I had what Dr. W. harris used to call an
"<u>aperçu</u>" namely the appropriation by the individualistic movement in politics, economics, religion of psychology was an intellectual calamity of a high order.
What might and should have been a chief instrumentality
in understanding the relations of human beings to one
another - the kind of understanding that nowhere had
the consequences in human activities that the new physical understanding had on technological activities....
(refers to) a positive disorientation which has been
very disruptive of reaching understanding - agreement
and highly provocative of misunderstandings and con-
flicts. For psychology to recover thorough going sen-
sitivity to <u>human</u> relationships as the proper suste-
nance is the only way he can take <u>human</u> advantage of
the immense gains in physical and technological mat-
ters. So three lusty cheers for <u>all</u> psychology is
social psychology. "We uns" ought to get together. We
must learn how to gang up and <u>give</u> a small scale demon-
stration of social psychology in operation.

Affectionately,

John Dewey

What the present world needs is a Declaration of Dependence. The Declaration of Independence is completely bankrupt. Hang together or hang separately is
more to the point now than in 1776. Staint [sic]
Benjamin Franklin situation and transaction are the
foci of the philosophical ellipse. But most I tell
believe a circle is superior to an ellipse not to mention even under the breath parabola.

93

December 13, 1950

Dear Earl [J. Kelley]:

.....What you say about the "dignity of the individual"
is of course true. But Wm. James somewhere pointed out
the uncivilized character of a civilization which sends
women and children to work fourteen hours a day in
underground holes in order to get what is called a
"living," saying nothing about an _effective_ opportunity
to share in the values that make the living worth much.

Appeal to the "intrinsic dignity of the individual" has
been used by vested institutional interests - industrial, political, religious - to cast a rosy glow over
practices in which there is no provision for creation
of conditions that will assure human beings a reason-
ably assured chance of life even half way dignified.
It's this substituting a pure abstraction for the concrete human being that got my goat.

How much does a social group that spends more of its
organized funds on war than a humane education care for
the dignity of the individual?.....I've got sort of
super-sensitive to the extent to which philosophy has
been used in this game of casting a rosy glow by what
is inhuman and discreditable as cover to protect vested
class and institutional interests.....

                              Affectionately,

                              John D.

                              Honolulu
                              Hawaii

                                             January 22, 1951

Dear Earl [J. Kelly]:

.....The names of Max Otto and Boyd Bode would probably
stand at the top of my list.....Am sure the chapter on
freedom [in your book] will be a corker.....Life here
is as free from tensions as it could be anywhere in the
present troubled world.

                              Yours most affectionately,

                              John Dewey

Los Angeles
California

March 8, 1951

Dear Earl [J. Kelly]:

.....It is a great support to me to know that a band of
fighters is active in carrying on the Good Fight - it's
a matter not of "progressive" education but of education itself - in which the belated revolution that will
enable mankind to realize.....the potentials of the
cultural and political revolution(s) has still to take
place. Maybe the time will come when we'll have reason
to be grateful even to Russia - for preventing us sink-
ing into the slough of complacency.

                    As ever yours affy.

                    John D. - and please give
                    my best to Rothman and the
                    others.

                    Los Angeles
                    California

                                        March 22, 1951

Dear Earl [J. Kelly]:

.....It will certainly be nice to see you and Rothman
in the flesh. Your letters have been a support to me
during my hospitalization. It will be the beginning of
a "new day" when I see you both in person.

                                        With love,

                                        John Dewey

1158 Fifth Avenue
New York 29, NY

June 27, 1951

Dear Earl [J. Kelly]:

.....I derive what comfort I can from the fact that
representatives of theological reaction find my position worthy of attack - even as far away as France
(referring to a French educational magazine) - but
after all what is needed is an organized positive co-
operative movement. If one can judge by Baker
Brownell's The Great Community, Northwestern University
should exert an increasingly helpful influence in the
years before us. For according to him the Great
Community consists of the face to face community of
outlook effort of ordinary folks. "In Union There is
Strength." E Pluribus Unum. The workshop idea (as
demonstrated in the book, Education for What is Real,)
as it becomes a fact presents the initiation of a new
epoch throughout the whole area of unforced and non-
coercive education.

                              Yours affy. as ever,

                              John Dewey

December 25, 1951

Dear Earl [J. Kelley]:

.....The human being simply <u>has</u> to <u>learn</u> in order to
live and his intercourse with others furnishes almost
automatically the conditions of this learning. Man is
pre-eminently <u>the</u> learning animal - only an imbecile
escapes and evades the process and he only by increase
of physical dependence on others.

Affectionately and gratefully yours,

John Dewey

Kilpatrick, William H. "John Dewey in American Life,"
    John Dewey and the Promise of America, Pro-
    gressive Education Booklet No. 14. Columbus,
    Ohio: American Education Press, Inc., 1939,
    pp. 5-11.

"My own opinion.....is that John Dewey is America come
to consciousness."

Even Kilpatrick confesses that, in his early contacts
with Dewey, "Somehow I did not get the hang of what he
said."

Clarence King
Box 1401
Nantucket, Mass. 02554

May 9, 1970

Dear Dr. Williams,

I greatly admired John Dewey but can be of no help because I had no contact with him. My college work was done at Wisconsin with two years of law at Columbia.

As perhaps you know, my 20 years of teaching at the New York School of Social Work were done when we were still at 22nd Street and I had very few contacts with the Columbia faculty.

Sorry not to help. Best wishes for your continued success.

Sincerely,

Clarence King

Herbert H. Lehman College
of the City University of New York
Department of Education
Bedford Park Boulevard West
Bronx, New York 10468

September 9, 1970

Dr. Robert B. Williams
Montclair State College
School of Education
Upper Montclair, NJ 07043

Dear Bob:

.....I have a piece on Dewey and "humanism" to be
published in a volume of selections from The Humanist.*
I enclose it, for the reference to Dewey in Fairfield's
introduction - I "reminisce" about Dewey in a letter to
R.P.F., the Editor of that volume.....

Best wishes for your publication.

Otto Krash

(*Dr. Krash refers here to: Roy P. Fairfield (Editor).
Humanistic Frontiers in American Education. Englewood
Cliffs, New Jersey: Prentice-Hall, 1971.)

315 West 106th Street, Apt. 15-C
New York, New York 10025

May 26, 1970

Professor Robert Bruce Williams
Associate Professor of Education
  and Social Work
Montclair State College
School of Education
Upper Montclair, NJ 07043

Dear Professor Williams:

I have received your letter of May 21 about my sending in some reminiscences of John Dewey.

However, practically all of my reminiscences of John Dewey went into the book I edited, <u>Dialogue on John Dewey</u>, published by Horizon Press in 1959.

Sincerely yours,

Corliss Lamont

CL:rc

Lamont, Corliss. Dialogue on John Dewey. New York:
        Horizon Press, 1959.

Horace Kallen:

I was in his seminar in ethics in the spring semester
of 1894; I'm probably the last survivor of that class.
(He's 86 now) It was from 4 to 6 p.m.; usually one or
another of the children would come in, open the door
and shout, 'John, are you ready to come home?' He nearly always managed to get rid of the kid or else bring
him up on the platform where the child remained a com-
petitor for the attention of the class. It was a warm
spring, a small class, and some of them were disre-
spectful enough to / snooze a little during the discussion, but Dewey didn't mind.....I think Dewey went to
Chicago the following autumn. - 17-18

Mrs. Agnes Meyer:

.....Dewey is the only one of whom I was continuously
in awe as a thinker and a personality. - 10

Herbert W. Schneider:

And all the years that I knew him in academic life his
conversation was confined largely to current issues and
what he called "the problems of men." - 16

[His ethics courses were] very interesting, because we
had systematic reading and unsystematic doctrine. - 16

Horace Kallen:

.....Turkey, Japan, China, Mexico, Israel, are all
places where the Dewey conception of education is
alive. I don't know how much impact it's had, but it's
definitely planted and is alive. - 129

Harold Taylor:

....no matter who said what, he encouraged the student
...../John made an honest effort to help everybody. -
33-34

John Herman Randall, Jr.:

He suffered fools gladly. - 34

February 14, 1972

Mr. Robert Bruce Williams
Professor of Education
Montclair State College
New Jersey, 07043

Dear Professor Williams:

The two Dewey letters (one minus contents) are enclosed.

I loaned my material to The Derrick and the Heritage
Society and the one letter was not returned.

You will note in letter of 1934, the reference of Oil
and Water.

Have at hand A Common Faith by John Dewey, which he
sent to my Dad* several years ago. Dad received
another one but when he passed away and the home was
sold, it disappeared.

The main topic when Dad and I talked about his former
teacher was: "Evolution-Darwin 'etc."

One thing I do remember is: "Dad blew up a test tube
experimenting on his own and Professor Dewey said.....
James, I should punch you on the nose but I'll charge
it to profit and loss."

No doubt, you have been in touch with John E. Selden re
John Dewey material. The late Colonel E.V.D. Selden,
his father, lived in the same boarding house when he
was single. He told me once that John Dewey was quiet,
conservative and a bit aloof, and didn't mix with the
other roomers.

John Dewey was a great American Philosopher and our
Heritage Society was going to place a plaque in his
memory but to my knowledge, nothing has been done.

We had a program at our Heritage Society in 1971 and it was well received.

Hope in a small way, the contents will be helpful. Please return all material. Thanks!

Sincerely yours,

Irene P. Lauffer
(Mrs. Martin J. Lauffer)

Enc. (4)

*J. Burrell Porterfield

Columbia University
in the City of New York
Department of Philosophy

1 W. 89
New York City

Jan. 3/40

Dear James [J. Burrell Porterfield]

It did me good to get your card as a reminder of
old days. You are one of the old "boys" I recall the
best. Do you remember the travelling wouldbe
scientist who could explain anything and you stumped
him by asking him why oil on stormy seas calmed the
waves?

I suppose you got my address from Mr. Selden.
With the best wishes for the New Year.

Sincerely your old friend

John Dewey

Mr. J. Burrell Porterfield (father of Irene Porterfield
154 West 3rd Street   Lauffer)
Oil City, PA

(Mr. Porterfield was a student of Dewey's when the
latter taught in the Oil City High School.)

MONTCLAIR STATE COLLEGE
Upper Montclair, New Jersey 07043

Dear Mrs. Lauffer:

How generous of you to write such a splendid
letter! This will be retyped for inclusion in the
volume on Dewey that we are now working on. I am
enclosing the excerpts from The Derrick, the empty
envelope from John Dewey under date of January 3,
1940, and the letter of January 3, 1940 to your father
from Professor Dewey.

Thank you for your kindness in letting us see
this very important material. The letter from Professor Dewey to your father will also form part of our
collection on Dewey recollections.

Again, my sincere thanks to you for your spendid
cooperation.

Very sincerely yours,

Robert Bruce Williams
Professor of Education
and Social Work

RBW:eb
Enclosures

Mrs. Martin J. Lauffer
Rt. 2 Stonecrest Manor
Oil City, PA 16301

February seventeen
1 9 7 2

IRENE PORTERFIELD LAUFFER
RD 2   Stonecrest Manor
Oil City, Penn'a. 16301

August 9, 1980

Dear Professor:

When the first High School was made into an ele-
mentary school, I also attended there. I am the
daughter of James Burrell Porterfield who tried a
laboratory experiment, and most blew up the place
(referring to Dewey's class in Natural Science). My
best wishes to you and your book on John Dewey.
Betsey Selden [daughter of Col. Selden] might contribute to this worthy cause. Her address: 14 Pinoak
Drive, Oil City, Pennsylvania 16301.

Very sincerely yours,

Mrs. Martin J. Lauffer
(Irene Porterfield Lauffer)

Lawrence, Nathaniel M. "Education as Social Process," in Charles W. Hendel (Editor). <u>John Dewey and the Experimental Spirit in Philosophy</u>. New York: The Liberal Arts Press, 1959.

Dewey was a visionary, and secular visionaires tend to be unduly optimistic. Human perversity, classically called "original sin" and equally obscurely known as "neurosis" or "psychosis," was never properly assessed by Dewey. He seems to have been what James called "once-born," the dark places of the human soul being little known to him. - 60

Leuchtenburg, William E. The Perils of Prosperity,
        1914-32. Chicago: The University of
        Chicago Press, 1958 - p. 46.

    Wilson and his intellectual supporters, such as
John Dewey, felt that this "most terrible and disas-
trous of all wars" could be countenanced only by de-
claring it the harbinger of eternal peace.

THE UNIVERSITY OF UTAH
SALT LAKE CITY   84112

October 21, 1970

Dear Professor Williams:

You may be interested in the following experience
which I had relative to Dewey back in the 30's.

Sometime in the middle 30's, I think
it was the summer of 1936, I traveled to
Logan, Utah with Professor E.E. Ericksen to
hear John Dewey address an evening gathering
of educators at Utah State University.

At the appropriate time Professor Dewey
was delivered at the outdoor theatre by a
young man of college age who had driven him
down from a home in Logan canyon where Dewey
was vacationing. After a round of introduc-
tions and handshaking I found myself in the
company of Dewey's host. In the course of
our conversation he suddenly said to me,
"Say, who is this man Dewey they're all making
such a fuss about?" As it turned out, the
young man's parents had invited Dewey to
vacation at their mountain home. Some time
after he arrived they had left for parts un-
known and their son was commissioned to
function as Dewey's host. He apparently
had little or no notion of who the great
man was.

If this tale, which is true, is of interest to
you, use it. I have no desire, however, to embarrass
the young man of the story, whose name I know but am
withholding.

Very sincerely,

Sterling M. McMurrin
Dean

SMM:hh/kg

112

MONTCLAIR STATE COLLEGE
Upper Montclair, New Jersey   07043

December 10, 1970

Dr. Robert B. Williams
Associate Professor of Education
Montclair State College
School of Education
Upper Montclair, NJ   07043

Dear Dr. Williams:

A former colleague of mine at the University of
Vermont - George Dykhuizen - who taught Intellectual
History - knew Dewey personally. (Dewey, as you
know, was born-'n-raised in Burlington, Vermont and
went to University of Vermont.) I also suggest a
most knowledgeable Dewey scholar, Philip Smith,
Chairman, Educational Foundations Department at the
University of Indiana. I knew Phil at the University
of Virginia; he did his dissertation on Dewey's pragmatism.

James Mehorter
Associate Professor of Education
Montclair State College

113

Mills, C. Wright. Sociology and Pragmatism: The
    Higher Learning in America. New York:
    Oxford University Press, 1966.

    An impression of Dewey in his last years at Michi-
gan from the standpoint of one who was his student runs
as follows:

    John Dewey, whose lectures on political
    philosophy I attended in 1893-94, certainly
    left a lasting mark, but rather by his
    personality, I think, than by this lectures
    ....his character was deeply admired, for
    its simplicity.....We believed that there
    was something highly original and significant
    in his philosophy, but had no definite ideas
    as to what it was. - 297

(Mills traces the above quotation to Charles H. Cooley,
"History of Department of Sociology at Michigan,"
Sociological Theory and Social Research (New York,
1930), p. 6.)

    The character of Dewey's contact [with Hull House,
Chicago] was not only that of a trustee but as a "warm
friend" and a "regular visitor." He participated at
least twice as a speaker. One of the problems that
occurs among immigrants is an estrangement of second
generation from the culture and, indeed, the persons of
the older generation.....About this [Jane Addams] had
many talks with Dr. Dewey. - 310-311

(Mills cites reference for Addams' talks with Dewey:
Jane Addams, Twenty Years at Hull House, With Auto-
graphical Notes. New York: Macmillan Company, 1910,
pp. 236-237.

    Dewey met Albert C. Barnes in 1915 in his seminar
at Columbia. The Art as Experience in 1934 is dedi-
cated to Barnes; Dewey's contact with the Barnes Foundation "gave philosophical form to his previously scattered ideas of the arts." - 318

(The quotation above is from Jane Dewey, The Philosophy
of John Dewey, p. 37.)

[Clarence E. Ayers] cites cases of Dewey's analytic ability, which he admires. - 321

In discussing Dewey's educational influence abroad, Mills refers to I.L. Kandel, "John Dewey's Influence on Education in Foreign Lands," in <u>John Dewey the Man and His Philosophy</u> (Cambridge, 1930), p. 71:

> Translations have appeared of practically all of his educational writings. One or more have been published in most of the European languages - French, German, Russian, Hungarian, Bulgarian, Greek, Italian, Spanish, and Swedish - and in Arabic, Turkish, Chinese, and Japanese, while special editions of his earlier works have been published in England - 334

Dewey presents a justification of science and philosophy in terms of their roles in facing this "supreme question." He does not deny a role to poetry. He states its function to be ethical and to lie within the limits of a "verifiable account of the universe." - 366

> Dewey once heard

> a physicist, quite innocent of the pragmatic controversy, remark that the knowledge of a mechanic or farmer was what the Yankee calls gumption - acknowledgement of things in their belongings and uses, and that to his mind natural science was only gumption on a larger scale: the convenient cataloguing and arranging of a whole lot of things with reference to their most efficacious services. - 398

We have seen the psychological reception given by Dewey to the thought of Hegel. It unified him and gave him a blend of "emotion and intellect" which he had not attained in any adolescent religion. - 443

MONTCLAIR STATE COLLEGE
Upper Montclair, New Jersey 07043

January 18, 1972

TO: Dr. Robert B. Williams

FROM: Dr. Earl E. Mosier

IN RE: Your "John Dewey: Recollections"

    John Dewey appeared [in the 30's] at the School-
masters Club at the University of Michigan a number
of times. The students had an opportunity to meet
with him after dinner. Those of us students so fortunate revered John Dewey the philosopher.

Nash, Paul, Kazamias, Andreas M., and Perkinson,
Henry J. The Educated Man: Studies in the
History of Educational Thought. New York:
John Wiley & Sons, Inc., 1965 - p. 304.

John Dewey (1859-1952) was born in Burlington,
Vermont, where his father was proprietor of a general
store. After receiving his bachelor's degree from the
University of Vermont, Dewey taught school in Oil City,
Pennsylvania, and later in a rural school in Vermont.
He left school teaching to pursue graduate studies at
Johns Hopkins University where he received his doctorate in 1884. That year he became instructor of philosophy at the University of Michigan. In 1888 he became
professor of philosophy at the University of Minnesota
but returned to occupy the university chair of philosophy at Michigan from 1889 until 1894. Thereafter for
ten years he headed the department of philosophy, psychology, and education at the University of Chicago and
from 1902 to 1904 served as director of the School of
Education. From 1904 until his retirement in 1930 he
was professsor of philosophy at Columbia University.
While at the University of Chicago, Dewey organized the
Laboratory School to test his educational ideas. He
first expressed these views on education in a series of
lectures, published as The School and Society in 1899.
This book was translated into almost every European
language as well as into Arabic and Japanese. After
becoming professor of philosophy at Columbia University, Dewey continued his interest in education by
lecturing at Teachers College and by the publication of
further books on education, How We Think, Experience
and Education, and Democracy and Education, his most
comprehensive work on education. During his years at
Columbia University, Dewey was invited to lecture in
Japan, in China where he stayed two years, and in
Mexico. He also made inspection tours of the schools
in Turkey and in the Soviet Union at the request of
these governments. Dewey's published books and articles include over 1,000 titles.

Nathan, Otto, and Norden, Heinz (eds.). <u>Einstein on Peace</u>. New York: Schocken Books, 1968 - pp. 112-113.

Einstein lent his support probably to none of those documents with greater enthusiasm than to the manifesto that was released on October 12, 1930, and represented an appeal against conscription and the military training of youth. It was signed by Einstein, Tagore, Romain, Rolland and many other fighters against wars, including Jane Addams, John Dewey, Upton Sinclair, Sigmund Freud, Auguste Forel, Thomas Mann, Stefan Zweig, Selma Lagerlof, H.G. Wells and Bertrand Russell.....

Nathan, Otto, and Norden, Heinz (eds.). Einstein on
          Peace. New York: Schocken Books, 1968 -
          pp. 424-425.

John Dewey, the aged philosopher and teacher, was
among those who received, in August 1947, an appeal
from the Emergency Committee of Atomic Scientists to
contribute to its work. Dewey replied to Einstein and
the members of the committee:[1]

I regret not to be able to contribute. I could
and would contribute if there were included in your
appeals all public statements and instructions given
your corps of lecturers concerning a definite movement
urging the repeal of the right of veto. I am not naive
enough to suppose the USSR would heed that appeal. But
at least there would be reason to hope that the money
would not be raised and spent in vain because of any
default for which the contributors were primarily re-
sponsible.

Einstein replied on September 4, 1947:

I thank you warmly for your kindness in writing to
me about the work of this committee. I am in full
agreement with your suggestion that our statements and
speakers should stress the practical necessity for the
repeal of the veto right.

I shall lay your proposal before the next meeting
of the trustees, which occurs in October, and hope that
they will concur.

Dewey replied on September 7, 1947:

Thank you heartily for your cordial response to my
suggestion. I am happy that you concur, and I deeply
prize your kind words.

With warm personal regards and appreciation of the
great work you are doing.

[1]The correspondence with John Dewey was made available
  through the courtesy of Mr. Harold Oram and is repro-
  duced by special permission of Mrs. John Dewey.

Neff, Frederick C. Philosophy and American Education. New York: The Center for Applied Research in Education, Inc., 1966 - p. 69.

John Dewey survived William James by over forty years, and we are likely to forget that the two were at one time contempories. Yet each contributed to occasional corrections in the other's thinking, and they were personal friends.

March 21, 1977

Dr. Robert Bruce Williams
Professor of Education and Social Work
Montclair State College
Upper Montclair, New Jersey 07043

Dear Bob:

I first became acquainted with the writings of John
Dewey through courses and seminars I took with Boyd H.
Bode at the Ohio State University. After completing a
master's degree with Bode, I enrolled in a doctoral
program at UCLA and eventually chose to concentrate on
the educational thought of Dewey and Bode in my disserta-
tation study. On the occasion of Dewey's ninetieth
birthday UCLA, along with many other colleges and uni-
versities around the world, marked the event with a
number of addresses outlining his contributions to the
fields of philosophy, psychology, education, sociology,
and law. I was invited to present his contributions to
education.

A short time later my address was published in the
California Journal of Secondary Education, and I mailed
Dewey a copy. He was kind enough to reply in the letter I am enclosing. A year or so later I found a message that had been placed there the day before in my
apartment box in Hollywood. It read, "Please call Mrs.
Dewey at the Teris Hotel. If not in, please state when
and where you may be reached." I made a perfunctory
call to the hotel and was informed by the operator that
"they" had left the day before for Arizona. When I
asked who "they" were, the operator consulted her re-
cords and said, "Mr. and Mrs. John Dewey." I almost
dropped the telephone when I heard this, for I had
supposed the message might have come from a friend of
my family back east. And so I missed the opportunity
of meeting Dewey by one day. "By the way," said the
operator, "who is he? They've had a lot of visitors
and phone calls." When I told her that John Dewey was
no less than America's greatest living philosopher, she
replied, "Well, I read a lot but I never heard of him."

121

A day or two later I received a typewritten letter
(since lost) from Dewey on Teris Hotel stationery. I
am sure he typed it himself because the typing was so
bad. When he came to the end of a line he just chopped
a word in two with no regard for syllables.

I cite the call from the Deweys as an example of the
humanity and democracy that Dewey lived. Had I known
that Dewey was in the vicinity, it would have been
quite natural for me to have sought him out. But here
was I, an obscure graduate student, being sought out by
Dewey. After that, as Bode would have said, I wouldn't
have called the Queen my aunt.

                                        Cordially yours,

                                        Frederick C. Neff

J.J. Oppenheimer
2318 Saratoga Dr.
Louisville, KY 40205

September 5, 1970

Re: Dr. John Dewey

1. I never had a class with John Dewey but I used to
    visit his classes once in a while, while I was a
    student at Teachers College. Of course he was
    "across the street," on Columbia University's cam-
    pus. I was impressed by the way he taught. He'd
    take up a concept or a word and work out the mean-
    ings especially unique meanings and applications.
    He impressed me as thinking out loud. There was a
    lot of discussion especially on his part. It was
    an amazing experience for me.

2. In the late thirties while Dr. Orville Brim of Ohio
    State and I were attending a curriculum meeting at
    Minneapolis we met Dr. Dewey by chance in a hotel
    lobby. Dr. Brim had had work with Dr. Dewey. So
    he introduced me to Dr. Dewey. I was especially
    impressed by his simple, unassuming, even modest
    manner of answering serious professional questions.
    And in appearances, he might have been a small town
    New England businessman. But after exchange of
    pleasantries, Dr. Brim asked him about the progress
    that had been made in elementary education. Dr.
    Dewey replies: "Oh, Dr. Brim, you know far more
    about that than I do. I have not followed elemen-
    tary education in any serious way since my experi-
    ences with my little school at the University of
    Chicago."

3. In the twenties while I was Dean at Stephens Col-
    lege, Columbia, Missouri, President James M. Wood
    had the habit of inviting distinguished foreigners
    to his home on the campus. At that time the German
    philosopher, Count Keyserling was making a great
    impression in some academic circles in the United
    States. At the dinner table one evening at Presi-
    dent Wood's our famous guest suddenly asked all of
    us who in the American scene would make a distinct
    contribution to culture in the next 50 or 100 years.

123

A number of nominations were made. When it came my
turn, I said "John Dewey." At that the huge,
rather tall than huge, Count said: "I met John
Dewey last week at my lecture at Columbia University. Surely that "little scrimp" couldn't add
anything to human knowledge." .....Later by several
weeks <u>Time</u> magazine had a short article on the
departure of the Count and the reporter asked the
Count what three things had the United States made
to civilization. The Count replied: "Jazz, sky-
scrapers (?) and John Dewey."

So very good to hear from you. Good luck with
your publication.

Cordially,

J.J.O.

241 La Roche Avenue
Harrington Park, NJ
June 10, 1970

Dear Mr. Williams,

    I don't know if you've heard of the Barnes Founda-
tion in Marion, Pennsylvania. This houses the art
collection of the late Dr. Alfred Barnes which is used
to instruct students in seeing art as experience. Dr.
Barnes and Miss Violette de Mazia, the present director
of the foundation, were friends, as well as disciples,
of John Dewey. Dr. Barnes, the late, was the author of
the text used in the course <u>The Art in Painting</u>,
Harcourt, Brace and World, Inc., 1925 whose dedication
is to John Dewey.....

                        Yours truly,

                        Mrs. Richard Ottaviano

Park, Joe (Editor). <u>The Philosophy of Education.</u>
        Second Edition. New York: The Macmillan
        Company, 1963.

Dewey has been called the greatest educational
philosopher since Plato. - 95

May 5, 1970

TO: Dr. Robert B. Williams

FROM: Dr. Earl K. Peckham

In response to your interest in gathering recollections of John Dewey, I have a burning personal recollection which took place about thirty-five years ago,
one evening in a classroom in Macy Hall, Teachers
College, Columbia University.

Dewey was speaking slowly and very carefully, also
in simply constructed sentences, which was typical of
his style. I was listening intently to a point. Many
of the class seemed to have left the area of thought.
Dewey himself seemed to have left, to have gone into
his own world. I felt that I was with him regardless
of the seeming absence of the other members of the
class. He hesitated after his point was made, and he
looked at me through his thick bifocals. I said to him
in a too loud, nervous voice, "Doesn't emotion play a
part in this thought process?" His stare fixed on me.
I was embarrassed. He was silent--then he walked slowly over to the window and looked into the night, for
the better part of two minutes. Then he looked back
and fixed his stare on me (at least that is how I felt)
and he said in a very slow and almost inaudible voice -
but he knew I heard and he seemed to me not to care if
anyone else heard or not - "Knowledge is a small cup of
water floating on a sea of emotion."

Houston Peterson, Ph.D.
4LW, 1 Washington Square Village
New York, NY   10012

January 4, 1972

Professor Dewey was scheduled to give an address at
Cooper Union, New York City, on Sunday evening,
December 7, 1941. Dewey had not heard of the war news
until two or three hours before the 8:15 lecture. He
proceeded with a rather full set of notes, and the
audience listened carefully - with the deepest respect,
(I felt) on that fateful night. There were probably
1500 or 1600 people present, nearly a full house.

Pounds, Ralph L. The Development of Education in
Western Culture. New York: Appleton-Century-
Crofts, 1968.

Dewey himself was a mild-mannered, soft-spoken
individual who was not an effective speaker. His writings are very difficult to understand; consequently,
many of Dewey's ideas have been interpreted and extended through his followers. Some of these disciples did
go at different tangents. Boyd Bode of Ohio State
University stressed Dewey's ideas of democracy as a
"way of life." John Childs of Teachers College, Columbia, was considerably interested in social philosophy
and in political applications of the pragmatic philosophy. William H. Kilpatrick who also taught for a
number of years in the Teachers College, Columbia, was
very strongly interested in the "project" method and it
is likely that certain extreme interpretations of Kilpatrick may have been more influential in the progressive education movement than the direct interpretation
of Dewey's own writing and thinking. - pp. 211-212

Wayne State University
Detroit, Michigan

July 17, 1963

While the author was serving as visiting professor at
Wayne State University, he was fortunate in meeting Dr
Helen Powell (Los Angeles State College), also a visit
ing professor at Wayne State University. Dr. Powell
was recalling a conversation she had with Dr. Bob
Rothman. The latter noted the Deweys in a New England
resort dining room, and observed that Dewey himself ha
been making notes on a magazine and putting it in his
pocket. Rothman thought to himself, "There is that
great man putting together some thoughts for a paper o
a book." With some hesitation, he approached Dewey,
only to learn that he was working on a double-crostic
puzzle.

Ratner, Sidney, and Altman, Jules (Editors). <u>John Dewey and Arthur F. Bentley</u>. New Brunswick, New Jersey: Rutgers University Press, 1964, p. 51.

November 5, 1932

My dear Professor Dewey:

While you were at Chicago, I had a place at the outer edge of one of your courses where I secured a certain manner of vision which.....I have long regarded as one of the three or four most valuable aids I have received. I am permitting myself to send you a copy of.....<u>Linguistic Analysis of Mathematics</u>.....With the strongest wishes for success in your present political work.

Sincerely yours,

Arthur F. Bentley

(This is part of an extensive collection of correspondence between Dewey and Bentley, appearing in this volume.)

Dear Bentley:

.....I wish I knew more physics. This damn individual-social business must be linked with the discrete-continuity. As far as I can get is that, no matter how extensive the field, observation is so centered that a certain discreteness or "nuclear" quality belongs to its material. While reasoning (discourse that is ordered) is like radiation or continuous wave motion. Maybe this is a crazy notion.....

John Dewey

<u>Ibid</u>., p. 74.

Harvard University
Department of Social Relations
William James Hall 280
Cambridge, Massachusetts 02138

26 May 1970

Mr. Robert Bruce Williams
Montclair State College
Upper Montclair, New Jersey   07043

Dear Mr. Williams:

I am not exactly a friend, a former student or a fellow teacher of John Dewey, but I had several chances to see him in situations which may have been somewhat unusual, and I thought I'd mention these in a note.

My parents were close friends--among few--of the late Dr. Albert C. Barnes who came to see me when I was a senior in Harvard College and wanted me to spend the next year traveling around Europe buying paintings with him. I liked and admired his collection (a few items of which now hang in our home in Cambridge) but I felt I knew nothing about art or the issues involved..... I remember one day he came and yanked me out of bed and said, "Let's go see Jack." "Jack" was of course, John Dewey. He took me over to John Dewey who was lecturing at Harvard and slapped him on the back and did so with a whack that I thought would send him across the room. He introduced us and we talked briefly. And there have been several other such occasions at college that year of 1930-31, but between Barnes' rambunctiousness, Dewey's shyness, and my own inability to relate to the two men when they were with each other, I had little to say to Dewey and little to recall from the meetings.

That summer I went to the Soviet Union, wrenched my knee working on a collective farm, had my head shaved and was given a pair of crutches in a Soviet hospital, and got myself onto one of the German Line boats, the Bremen or the Europa, to come back to Harvard in September, 1931. It turned out that John Dewey was on the boat and a few other intellectuals who were friends of his, and a girl who was rather looking after him--a very attractive younger woman whose name I don't recall. "Jack" here was enormously relaxed. He was much interested, of course, in the USSR and we

132

talked about that, but mostly it was simply social and
pleasant and light--enormously so. John Dewey was gay
in a way I had not expected. On crutches myself I
could not have danced, and I don't know whether John
Dewey did or not, but he was in the spirit to do so.

Even then I had an interest in education and had
brought to Harvard to speak a number of educators, such
as Alexander Meiklejohn, Clarence Cook Little and
others. But I don't recall ever talking about education with John Dewey.

I don't know whether such fragmentary and perhaps
not entirely accurate vignettes are of use to you. I
never saw John Dewey again so far as I recall, although
I very much was on his side in his battles over the
purges and over Trotsky and so on in the 1930's and
later.

Sincerely,

David Riesman

DR:nm

Harvard University
Department of Social Relations

William James Hall 280
Cambridge, Massachusetts 0213&

9 June 1970

Professor Robert Bruce Williams
Montclair State College
Upper Montclair, New Jersey 07043

Dear Professor Williams:

    I don't know of anybody who called John Dewey
"Jack" except Albert C. Barnes, and he may have done it
only to show off on occasion.....

                           Sincerely yours,

                          David Riesman

DR:nm

Runes, Dagobert (ed.). Treasury of Philosophy.
    London: Peter Owen Ltd., 1955 - pp. 328-329.

Dewey, John (1859-1952). At the celebration of
his ninetieth anniversary, John Dewey declared that
losing faith in our fellow men means losing faith in
ourselves, "and that is the unforgivable sin." Dewey
is generally recognized as America's leading philosopher, and the foremost apostle of the faith in the
essential union of the democratic and philosophical
spirit. Since his revolt against German philosophy, he
repudiated the separation of the individual and the
social, both of which, according to him, are concrete
traits and capacities of human beings. He always regarded reason, not as something existing timelessly in
the nature of things, but simply as a fortunate and
complex development of human behavior. His criticism
of the traditional notions of truth is embodied in his
theory of instrumentalism, which he defines as "an
attempt to constitute a precise logical theory of concepts, judgments and inferences in their various forms,
by primarily considering how thought functions in the
experimental determinations of future consequences."
Dewey made inquiry, rather than truth or knowledge, the
essence of logic.

Russell, Bertrand. <u>The Autobiography of Bertrand
        Russell, 1914-1944</u>. New York: Little, Brown
        and Company, 1968 - pp. 174, 187-188, 364-365
        366.

     The Tuchun* gave a magnificient banquet, at which
we first met the Deweys, who behaved with great kindness, and later, when I became ill, John Dewey treated
us both with singular helpfulness. I was told that
when he came to see me in the hospital, he was much
touched by my saying, "We must make a plan for peace"
at a time when everything else that I said was
delirium.

*The military Governor of the Province

                         6 Yu Yang Li
                         Avenue Joffre
                         Shanghai, China
                         6th Oct. (? Nov.) 1920

Dear Sir:

.....Since 1919, the student's circle seems to be the
greatest hope of the future of China;.....In that year,
Dr. John Dewey had influenced the intellectual class
with great success.....

                         Your Fraternally Comrade,
                         Johnson Yuan
                         (Secretary of the Chinese
                         Anarchist-Communist Asso-
                         ciation)

                         (Permanent address)
                         Little Datchet Farm
                         Malvern, R.D. 1, Pa.; U.S.A.
                         January 18th 1941

My dear Gilbert [Murray]:.....

     I am giving a 4-year course of lectures on history
of philosophy in relation to culture and social circum-
stances, from Thales to Dewey.....

                         Yours ever,
                         Bertrand Russell

Russell, Bertrand. A History of Western Philosophy.
        New York: Simon and Schuster, 1945 - p. 819.

    John Dewey, who was born in 1859, is generally
admitted to be the leading living philosopher of
America. In this estimate I entirely concur. He has
had a profound influence, not only among philosophers,
but on students of education, aesthetic and political
theory. He is a man of the highest character, liberal
in outlook, generous and kind in personal relations,
indefatigable in work. With most of his opinions I am
in almost complete agreement. Owing to my respect and
admiration for him, as well as to personal experience
of his kindness, I should wish to agree completely, but
to my regret I am compelled to dissent from his most
distinctive philosophical doctrine, namely the substi-
tution of "inquiry" for "truth" as the fundamental
concept of logic and theory of knowledge.

    Like William James, Dewey is a New Englander, and
carries on the tradition of New England liberalism,
which has been abandoned by some of the descendants of
the great New Englanders of a hundred years ago. He
has never been what might be called a "mere" philosopher. Education, especially, has been in the forefront
of his interests, and his influence on American education has been profound. I, in the lesser way, have
tried to have an influence on education very similar to
his.   Perhaps he, like me, has not always been satis-
fied with the practice of those who professed to follow
his teaching, but any new doctrine, in practice, is
bound to be subject to some extravagance and excess.
This, however, does not matter so much as might be
thought, because the faults of what is new are so much
more easily seen than those of what is traditional.

January 26, 1972

To: Dr. Robert B. Williams

From: Professor George E. Salt

In Re: Your "John Dewey: Recollections."

My recollection of John Dewey (in the thirties at Northwestern University, as a guest speaker) was of him entering the classroom, sitting behind the desk, opening the left-hand bottom drawer, putting his feet up, gazing out of the window, and beginning to talk about reality without looking at the students. He would say,

> "There are things we observe out there, but how do we know that they are existential?"

Then he launched into the pragmatic implications. He kept glued to the window constantly instead of looking at the students. I was already oriented toward philosophical thinking, but Dewey stimulated further my interest in the area.

GES:eb

Schneider, Herbert. "Recollections of John Dewey,"
    Claremont Quarterly, 11 (Winter 1965), 23-
    35.

RECOLLECTIONS OF JOHN DEWEY
by Herbert Schneider

Schneider: Dewey didn't lecture. He talked largely to
himself and to God and looked out of the window, and we
were usually--it was after lunch--hard put to it to
keep awake, but when we read our notes afterwards we
realized that we had been listening to some very extraordinary lecturing, but his manner was very informal
and not lecturing at all. He was almost always thinking out a problem for himself. I can give you one
illustration. He would come to class with a small
sheet of paper which he would then crumple up gradually
as he talked. By the end of the lecture it would be
just a little wad of paper that he would stick in his
pocket or throw in the wastebasket. One day he was
working on criteria for culture. The problem he was
working on was whether there was any way we could judge
cultures relative to each other. How would you decide
whether a culture is good or not? After a lot of fum-
bling around with more or less formal systems of sociology, he said, "What I am driving at, I guess, is that
the best way to estimate the quality of a culture is to
see what kind of people are in its jails." That was
typical of his way of going at it. The failures would
usually stimulate him more than the successes because
they were the real problematics in existence. He would
begin with frustrations and failures and those things
that made interests problematic. Not only his lecturing but his whole educational program was focused on
that.

Hutchison: What about Dewey's relation to students?
Was he a warm and friendly person? Or was he so preoccupied with his own ideas that he didn't have time for
students?

Schneider: The two things worked together. He had an
amazing quality for making friends without making disciples. Although a good many of his students turned
out to be disciples, it wasn't anything he wanted or
aimed at. His whole manner in the classroom was anti-
professional educator. I remember one day toward the
end when he said, "If I go down in history at all, I

want to go down in history as a philosopher and not as an educator. I don't feel that I am a professional educator. In general this whole education business is apt to be misrepresented because I think that the teacher, so-called, shouldn't regard himself so much as a teacher as a helper or an assistant in helping an individual work out his own interests to his own satisfaction, so that a real teacher will go to a child or adult and say, "What is it that you are thinking about and what would like to have in the way of help?"

Whenever we went into Dewey's office, he always took that attitude: What are you working at? What sort of difficulty do you have? What sort of reading would you like? I remember in my own case I thought at first it was just his kindness to me but I found out that it was his general technique. I think it was partly strategy and partly just his good democratic nature because he was extremely democratic, not only in theory, but also in practice. When he came in, he would say, "Have you got anything written that you want to show me?" If we had, he would immediately read it. I remember one little essay I wrote--I think it was my first year in graduate school--on Rousseau's Social Contract, and I had entitled it "Mathematical Method in Rousseau," which just meant that he could find the general will by definition. Dewey read that and said, "I had never thought of this in this way. You've got something there. You'd better work it out." He did that with almost all of his students. In the dissertation, too, he continually worked at fine points in the problem, and he was always encouraging.

When he gave a seminar to a group of eight or ten, we had a thoroughly cooperative problem to work out. I had one seminar with him on Group Ethics, which was quite interesting. Each student had to take some group and work out the ethics that the group had worked out for itself. It was very experimental. I had another seminar with him on John Stuart Mill's Logic. In the seminars he didn't lecture at all. He just listened and criticized the students.

Hutchison: What you were saying a moment ago about Dewey not wanting to go down either as a professional educator or as a man who made disciples seems to me ironical in the light of the Deweyism which has been picked up and become a kind of philosophy of education in many parts of the country. What would he have thought of that?

140

Schneider: His chief interest was to break down the
wall of separation between school and society, and he
wanted to have the same general atmosphere in school
that you have in the so-called cold external world of
affairs and make the school a school in which there
were "affairs"--he liked to use that word--being conducted. He tried his best not to make them play affairs, not to play store or play house or play this and
that, but actually to conduct some serious cooperative
enterprise. He insisted that these be cooperative
enterprises and that the teacher be party to the cooperation. That was not always easily carried out but
that was his theory and as best he could he applied
that theory. It came rather naturally to him because,
as I say, he was habitually very democratic and helpful.

Beatty: You say in this little book called Dialogue on
John Dewey that "Dewey liked a non-academic atmosphere
better than any other philosopher that I know." Could
you give us more examples of this?

Schneider: At the same time as he was giving courses,
he was taking part in all sorts of cultural activities
outside of school, and during the war years he was in
politics a great deal. He was writing for the New
Republic on current public affairs. He was helping
organize the so-called People's Lobby in Washington to
have the people's interest as a special pressure group.
After the first World War he worked hard to prevent
Paderewski and a group of Polish imperialists from
taking over Poland. Then he spent a good deal of time
on the Trotsky trials, criticizing them, and he was
very active in comtemporary politics. He was also
interested in the arts but with one exception. He was
tone deaf and couldn't appreciate music. He would go
to concerts with friends but he wouldn't enjoy them.
He had a great interest in poetry and painting and
himself wrote some poetry, but did no painting. He
appreciated those two arts.

Hutchison: Where would you place Dewey in the political spectrum? I ask this question particularly because
I think he has been libeled perhaps in recent times.

Schneider: He called it the "New Individualism" but it
was in practice a kind of what the Germans would call
"Social Democracy." He was very close to the Fabian
Socialists, the Guild Socialists in England. He wanted
to avoid bureaucracy and state socialism, but he

141

thought any movement which would help to institutional-
ize, or as he used to say "to vest," public interest
and give it power as a pressure group was all to the
good, and his chief aim was to scold those attempts of
government which create barriers to communication or
set up closed groups of experts. His great aim was to
promote what Graham Wallace called the "open society"--
Bergson, too--and avoid all rigid party and rigid class
distinction.

Hutchison: You remember Dewey as a colleague as well
as a teacher; do you have any particular recollections
of his qualities and limitations as a colleague?

Schneider: I was associated with him very closely for
many years from 1920 to 1940, and after his retirement.
He attended to his academic duties very well and intel-
ligently but also very informally. For a year or two
he was executive officer of the department and he usually conducted it all by writing postcards. He seldom
used a secretary. He did the department work effec-
tively but in the most informal way. In general he
tried to avoid red tape wherever he could. He was very
well liked as a colleague, had many friends in the
faculty, chiefly in other departments. He didn't cultivate his fellow philosophers very much, and he was on
much more intimate terms with some of the people in
politics, sociology, history, the social sciences in
general. He didn't have much interest in natural
science.

Hutchison: I have heard it said that he was terribly
absent-minded. Is that a correct impression?

Schneider: He gave the impression of being absent-
minded but you seldom caught him at being irresponsi-
ble. Once in a while he would forget an engagement but
usually he was quite punctilious and he went out of his
way to be responsive to groups, individuals who asked
him to speak. He did this right up to the end even
when it was physically very hard for him to appear in
public. He still accepted--when students asked him, or
some organization asked him--as a favor, not for money.
He hated to lecture for money, but he would do it as a
friendly act.

Hutchison: What about his family?

Schneider: The first Mrs. Dewey was an ardent feminist
and began that in the Michigan days, and Dewey was

142

quite interested in the whole system of women's rights from the start, but she took the initiative. There are many stories about her using him in many ways in women's parades and so on. He was quite jubilant when women won their voting rights. But in many other ways he allowed Mrs. Dewey to work with him and in many ways to take the lead. She was quite a leader and aggressive, and he didn't seem to mind that at all. But the school at Chicago thought that she was interfering more with the running of the School of Education than they wanted, although I don't know the details. One reliable story is that it was Mrs. Dewey's interference with the School of Education more than his own policies that led to the rupture there. After he got to New York when I knew him, Mrs. Dewey kept out of academic affairs. She had her own interests, political and social. They had tea parties once a week to which students and colleagues were invited. They were very informal and very pleasant.

When Mrs. Dewey died, for quite a number of years he lived with his children in an apartment, and we saw a good deal of him in those days. During the summer he would go out to the seashore, to a farm he had on Long Island. He was extremely sociable in this democratic sense. Almost always if we went to his house for a party or any occasion that he managed, we met with a great number of people outside of academic life. He had many more friends outside of academic circles than inside--civil rights, labor unions, journalists. One of his very close friends was Albert Barnes, who was a collector of art and got interesteed in the theory of art largely through Dewey. He and Dewey cooperated in a book on Art as Experience. Dewey was very much engrossed for a number of years in this philosophy of art with Barnes. In his own life I think he carried out better than in the classroom his belief that there should be no separation between school and outside.

Hutchison: You have spoken about his ethical and social interests. Very frequently one hears the charge made that Dewey was anti-religious or irreligious. Would you want to speak to this as you knew him?

Schneider: He was irreligious in the sense that he wasn't interested in any particular religion. He reminisced only once in a while--it was very difficult to get him to reminisce of his childhood. We know that during the Michigan days he was a Sunday School teacher and was active in church affairs there and Y.M.C.A.

He said, "My religion I got from Coleridge when I was
in Vermont. His <u>Aids to Reflection</u> and in general his
approach to conventional religion was a real godsend to
us because it enabled us to think about the spirit and
things of the spirit without getting sentimental or
supernatural or doctrinaire and using it just as a term
without knowing what we meant by it. For Coleridge and
for us spiritual religion meant something quite different, meant something liberating and liberating from
both conventional religion and from atheism." He said,
"I've not changed my religious opinion but I've quit
talking about it because I can't find anybody who is
interested in it beside myself."

     When he came to write those lectures at Yale which
were published as "A Common Faith," he didn't want to
write them at all but after he had written a couple of
them he called me in one day and said, "I wish you
would read this first chapter." I noticed at once that
he was going out of his way to talk about religion
without talking about any particular religion. He was
actually condemning institutionalized religion. He
said religion should be a quality of life and not institutionalized. I talked to him about that. He said,
"I want this to be a very common faith, very common."
He had the notion that religion should be something
very close to everyday life and not something apart in
an institution.

Hutchison: I was going to ask you about some of the
basic ideas of Dewey's philosophy. Certainly the ideas
of nature and naturalism were as basic to his thoughts
as any of them. Would you want to comment further on
his view of nature and naturalism? It certainly wasn't
a reductive idea in any sense of the word?

Schneider: No, I think it is rather misleading to call
him a naturalist because we identify that with the
natural sciences and the only natural science he was
really interested in was biological psychology. He
took a biological approach to practically everything--
ethics, politics, and so on. But otherwise his interests were cultural and not related to the natural
sciences. The social sciences were central in his
whole life but he made the scientific method his real
passion, you might say, and tried to insist that it's
the method and not the subject matter that's important.

Hutchison: What then did he mean by "nature"?

Schneider: He never told you! I don't think he had a
theory of nature at all. I tried to work out a few
pages on nature; he read it and the first thing he said
was,"You don't take nature philosophically enough." I
never found out what he meant by a philosophy of nature. I think for him nature was simply a convenient
term for all there is. It was a substitute for reality. He thought man should be studied as a natural
emergence and in his natural environment. He wanted
society to be one complex of what he called "human
activity."

Hutchison: Among the other ideas that Dewey expressed
is the idea of intelligence. How has that stood up in
the years?

Schneider: That makes me want to say something about
his relation to Progressive Education because when
Progressive Education itself became a movement, a more
or less polemical movement, Dewey and his eldest daughter, Evelyn, were the first, I think, to write a critical estimate of the value of Progressive Education as
it was actually being conducted. I remember his saying, "I am in great sympathy with the aims of these
people but they don't know how to go about it because
they forget that the chief aim of education is to make
people intelligent. My whole interest in education and
in democracy, for that matter, is to stimulate intelligence in anybody and everybody. If education doesn't
make people intelligent, there is no point in it." So
he wanted the so-called "progressive" methods in education focused around the discipline of interests. He
insisted--and this was, of course, what caused a good
deal of the theoretical trouble--that you have to start
with actual interests. You don't create interests.
You find them, and then you try to cultivate an interest so as to make it an intelligent interest. It's the
transformation of what he called idle curiosity into
intelligent concern that was his basic program for
education. "The trouble with progressive educators is
that they have lost this main drive of disciplining
interest. They cater to interests." He blamed Montessori for a good deal of that. He said they don't dis-
tinguish between my ideas and Montessori's pampering
natural interests.

Hutchison: How well do you think Dewey in general has
stood up through the decades?

Schneider: There was a reaction against Dewey for a short time. He was attacked from both extremes, if I might call it that. Marxians attacked him as not taking the class struggle seriously enough, and that's perfectly true. He didn't take class struggle seriously because he didn't take classes seriously. He wasn't interested in the European social analysis but largely American and he didn't think classes were what the Europeans represented them to be in this country, so that his liberalism was adapted more to an analysis of American society than to European.

Beatty: He did take an interest in the Trotsky trials, though. What got him interested in that?

Schneider: Because he realized that Trotsky was being misrepresented by the Stalinists. He was pushed into this by Sidney Hook, but he was quite willing to be pushed into it because he thought it was an outrageous misrepresentation. He wasn't a Trotskyite the way Sidney Hook was. Dewey never was a doctrinaire Socialist but he took Socialism very seriously because he thought the Socialists had the same general aim he had, at least the American Socialists. But he wasn't willing to formulate it as Marxian. So the Marxians jumped on him and on liberalism and said that liberalism was bourgeois. There was nothing bourgeois about Dewey. He was a Vermont Yankee and he kept a people-to-people attitude. There was nothing class conscious about him at all.

Then he was attacked by the clergy, who had grounds for attacking him, I think, because of his anti-theological bias. They said he just had a blind spot for all theological ideas, which is quite true. He more or less resented, I think, the revival of theology as being a disservice to religious and secular thinking.

Beatty: Was there any other one of the world religions that he might have been more sympathetic with?

Schneider: No, I don't think he took any interest in any religion.

Hutchison: He was an anti-organization man in the whole thing.

Schneider: In religion he was anti-organization, but he wasn't that in other affairs. On the contrary, he wanted to organize public interests, and his People's Lobby he took very seriously, theoretically. It fizzled out as a practical plan. Theoretically he thought that there was such a thing as the public interest, and the public interest deserved to have an institutionalized representation, and he was discouraged because Congress wasn't doing that.

Beatty: He wasn't active in the Progressive Education organization?

Schneider: No. He didn't want to condemn them, because they were being attacked for the wrong reasons. When they needed defense he would come to their defense, but he would at the same time criticize them in their own circles rather severely for not having the proper techniques.

Hutchison: It would be true, then, that in the philosophy of education Dewey is not a "Deweyan" or a "Deweyist."

Schneider: He doesn't have the doctrinaire attitude toward his philosophy that those who preach his philosophy as gospel have. This is a big difference. I said that I thought that the reaction against Dewey was temporary because now it seems to me that on the whole, at least in our philosophical circles, Dewey is taken quite seriously as one of the great thinkers of his time. But it is quite true that Dewey's language and the way he went at philosophy are no longer as important as for our generation.

Hutchison: This means that the situation is changing.

Schneider: Dewey, I think, would be the first to recognize that the situation today isn't the situation which he faced. He continually tried to keep abreast of the times and to conceive of the changing situation because he took change for granted.

Beatty: He would be happy, wouldn't he, about the accessibility of education for everyone today, about the increase in college enrollments?

Schneider: Oh yes, he tried to emphasize in his writings and even more in his talking that the idea that education goes on only in school is all wrong, that we are being educated all our lives, if we are educated at all, and that the school is merely an attempt to make

147

us aware of what it means to be in the process. To think that your education stops when your schooling stops is ridiculous. He said that these people who want to get out of school have the wrong idea.

Hutchison: In this respect as in others, Dewey is a kind of philosopher of democracy, isn't he?

Schneider: He was almost fanatical on that.

Beatty: In the book, Dialogue on John Dewey, one of the commentators spoke of Dewey as being the leading American philospher? How do you feel about that statement now?

Schneider: Being close to him, I wasn't aware of this at the time, although I knew that he had a great deal of influence. Those who write history now magnify his position. I don't know. I am not sure what to say, but if you were to ask "Whom would you put ahead of him?" I don't know. There were a group of philosophers who succeeded in making philosophy not only a serious field of study but also a kind of life. Dewey had an enormous influence but you mustn't underestimate the influence of people like James and Royce and half a dozen others.

Hutchison: At a minimum, though, he gave philosophical expression to some of the basic issues and ideas of the time in which he lived, didn't he?

Schneider: Yes, I think that's the heart of it. Much more than James, he philosophized--if we use that term--about the life in which he found himself. He had very little interest in historical study, although when he did it, it was usually quite interesting. It wasn't always accurate but it was stimulating. It was the life that was going on all around him that really preoccupied him.

Beatty: To what extent does the philosophy of education at Teachers College over the years reflect his influence?

Schneider: At the time I was there, his influence was still dominant but already it was being reshaped by Kilpatrick in the light of Progressive Education. We thought that Kilpatrick, although he had Dewey's ideas, exploited them and used them very differently from Dewey's own way. Dewey's own way of conducting a class was very different from Kilpatrick's.

Hutchison: Kilpatrick lectured and in an educational sense created "Deweyism," did he not?

Schneider: No, he made the class lecture to each other. Dewey wouldn't stand for that. Dewey was more critical. Kilpatrick stimulated what we call education by colloquium. Dewey wasn't interested in colloquium as such any more than he was interested in dialectic as such. I remember in his Group Ethics seminar he said to one student, "How do you explain this particular way of acting?" The student said, "I think it is just due to plain human laziness." Dewey jumped on him fiercely and said, "Don't you know better than to use laziness as a cause?" It was quite a technical point but I never saw him jump on anyone as hard as he jumped on that fellow. He was a very sharp critic although he was usually quite gentle in his manner. His writing is very polemical but Dewey personally wasn't a polemical person.

Hutchison: He had a good deal of interest in the history of ideas, did he not?

Schneider: He had an interest in it. His courses were continually using historical material. Part of his method was to show that philosophy had always been what he thought it should be.

Hutchison: Namely?

Schneider: Namely, an intelligent concern for genuine problems. One day he said, "I've just been reading G.E. Moore's autobiography. Moore admitted in print what I wouldn't expect anybody would admit. Moore wrote: 'I think that if I hadn't been reading other people's books, I wouldn't have had any problems.' That's a terrible confession."

Hutchison: Dewey was certainly sharp in his criticism of false problems of philosophers in contrast to the philosophical treatment of human problems.

Schneider: He entitled one of his collections of essays Problems of Men. He took it rather seriously because he thought we should recognize problems as actual and we shouldn't "cook up" artificial problems even for school room use. We should deal with actual problems, not manufactured.

149

WILLIAM K. SELDEN
50 Westcott Road
Princeton, NJ

August 11, 1980

Professor Robert Bruce Williams
48 Harrison Avenue
Roseland, New Jersey   07068

Dear Bob:

There is reference to Dewey's statement [as reported in the <u>News-Herald</u>, July 19, 1980] that men in the boarding house he resided, had suggested that he purchase stock in the Standard Oil Company of New Jersey. The men were my father, Edwin van D. Selden, and his older brother, Connor C. Selden.

Sincerely yours,

William K. Selden

Indiana University
Bloomington, Indiana 47401

June 25, 1970

Robert Bruce Williams, Ed.D.
Associate Professor of Education and
  Social Work
Montclair State College
School of Education
Upper Montclair, New Jersey 07043

Dear Dr. Williams:

My only contact with John Dewey consisted of attendance at an intersession seminar which he offered in the mid-1930's at the University of Cincinnati. At that time I was in my early 20's and probably not constituted to appreciate the man's wisdom and greatness as I later came to know him through his writings.

Actually, I found his lectures hard to follow in view of my limited background and drew comfort only in the fact that a number of my classmates also seemed to have difficulty in identifying with the great man's viewpoints. I think in retrospect that too many of us who were teachers enrolled simply because he was "a great man"--so that we could say that we had a course with him rather than because of any thirst for knowledge. As I recall the man, Professor Dewey seemed more interested in new ideas than in his under promising students. There was difficulty in following him because one had to concentrate closely on what he was saying lest they miss an important message in the wide-range comments which marked his presentations.

So you see, there is nothing I could do to be of help.

Sincerely,

Harold G. Shane
University Professor
  of Education

HGS:mm

Warren Allen Smith
94 Millport Avenue
New Canaan, Connecticut 06840

25 May 1970

Dear Mr. Williams:

John Dewey's own philosophic preference, of
course, is detailed in his books. He was, however, a
member of the American Humanist Association. When
pursuing my M.A. at Columbia in 1949, I formed the New
York Chapter of the A.H.A. and secured Dewey as the
first dues-paying member--in fact, I still have his
uncashed check. Later, as book review editor of The
Humanist, I received a ticket to and attended his
funeral. It's not clear to me what you could write
that has not already been written, but should you need
further information about Dewey's relationship to the
A.H.A. I would be willing to help.

Sincerely,

Warren Allen Smith

Faculty of Arts and Sciences
University of Pittsburgh
Pittsburgh, Pennsylvania 15213

June 9, 1970

Professor Robert Bruce Williams
Montclair State College
Upper Montclair, New Jersey   07042

Dear Professor Williams:

In a recent New York Times Book Review I read your
request for information about John Dewey.

On the occasion of his 90th birthday the late Dr.
Richard Hope, a former student of Dewey's, and I interviewed Dr. Dewey at his summer home near Pittsburgh.
The recording which we made has been called by some who
knew Dr. Dewey best a succinct and accurate statement
of his philosophy.

If you would be interested I could provide you
with a taped copy of the interview and a photocopy of a
handwritten letter which Dewey wrote to me about the
interview. My only charge would be for out of pocket
expenses in making copies. I'll be in Pittsburgh again
by Labor Day.

Cordially,

William S. Tacey, Ed.D.
Professor of Speech

Summer Address:
(June 15-September 1)

Waterford, Maine 04088

Faculty of Arts and Sciences
University of Pittsburgh
Pittsburgh, Pennsylvania 15213

July 7, 1970

Dr. Robert Bruce Williams
Associate Professor of Education
  and Social Work
Montclair State College
Upper Montclair, New Jersey 07043

Dear Dr. Williams:

Dewey's summer home was about as close to Greensburg as to New Alexandria. It originally belonged to
his second wife's family who manufactured glass in
Greensburg, and I believe that they used the address
there. It had an outdoor bathhouse which Mrs. Dewey
assured us that John used daily.

Although I have my masters degree from TC (Columbia U.), Dewey was not one of my teachers because he
had already retired. I studied at TC in the summers of
1929 to 1932. Of course, his influence there was still
great. Save for a course in labor relations offered on
the Columbia side of the campus, his name was mentioned
almost daily in other classes.

My acquaintance with Dewey was limited to three
visits to his summer home when he was ninety. At the
time he was frail physically, but as alert mentally as
ever.

Once I asked him if he still lectured occasionally. He replied, with a twinkle in his eye, "No, I just
had an invitation to go to the University of Chicago
for a week. I replied that I had two young children to
look after, and that they needed their father."

You doubtless know more about the adopted refugee
children (boy and girl) than I do. They were in about
the 10 to 12 year age range when I saw them.

Once as we walked to our car after a visit the
Deweys walked with us. The children were discovered
climbing a small ornamental tree, breaking branches as
they climbed. Mrs. Dewey reproved them sternly, and
ordered them back to the ground. Dr. Dewey nodded
approval, giving evidence, I thought, that his philosophy didn't mean that children should be allowed to do
exactly as they pleased, regardless of the consequences.

After we finished recording the interview for the
radio program which I mentioned, Dewey was avid to hear
the playback. He listened with great intentness, completely absorbed in what he was hearing. As the program ended, he turned to me and asked: "Professor
Tacey, I notice that in several places my voice isn't
as strong or as clear as it should be. What can I do
to improve it?"

I often cite the experience when a student says
that he is too old to make changes in his speech
habits.

At cocktail time I noticed that Dr. Dewey was
almost abstemious in his drinking habits. When our
need to drive to Pittsburgh was mentioned, Mrs. Dewey
assured us that the drinks were mixed to suit John's
needs and that we must have no fear of them.

Contrary to what I had always heard about the
dullness of Dewey's lectures, I found that in his conversation (which he tended to dominate in a group of
six to eight men and Mrs. Dewey) he had a sparkling
wit, directness in visual and vocal contact, and an
enviable ability to field questions quickly. His mental vigor for one of his years was outstanding, and he
demonstrated a broad knowledge of what was then current
in educational philosophy.

Have you heard about this incident which is supposed to have happened at his 90th birthday party at
the Waldorf-Astoria Hotel? A younger man on congratu-
lating him said: "Dr. Dewey, I hope that I'll be back
to help you celebrate your 100th birthday." Dewey,
tongue carefully tucked in cheek, answered: "You look
healthy to me, I think you ought to make it."

My principal recollection of Dr. Dewey is that he
was warm and outgoing, a man blessed not only with an
extremely fertile mind but a ready wit and a great
sense of humor. Mrs. Dewey, though then less than half
his age seemed to be deeply in love with him, and he
reflected that feeling.

I shall write at once to Dr. Boydston, as you
suggest.

                              Cordially,

                              William S. Tacey

Mailing address until September 1:

    Waterford, Maine   04088

The City College
                           of
              The City University of New York
                   New York, NY 10031

                                        June 17, 1970

Dear Mr. Williams:

     In 1932 I was an English graduate student at
Columbia. Ashley Thorndike was then Chairman of the
English Dept. and every graduate student took his
Shakespeare course, which came at 2 p.m. in a lecture
room holding over 100 - on the 6th floor of Philosophy
Hall. One day, promptly at 2 p.m. Professor Dewey
shambled in, sat down at the desk and proceeded to read
a long list, marking absent each one, since there was
no reply from a crowded room. At 2:10 Thorndike strode
into the room, gawped at Dewey a moment, then tapped
him on the shoulder, saying: "John, you are one flight
up." None of us laughed as Thorndike proceeded to read
the proof sheets of his Shakesperian Comedy.

     Good luck in your project.

                                   John C. Thirlwall
                                   Professor of English

Norman Unger
5545 Netherland Ave.
Riverdale, NY 10471

May 26, 1970

Dear Mr. Williams,

I'll never forget the picture when meeting Mr.
Dewey for the first time.

I wanted to have some of his books autographed, so
I called and he very kindly invited me to come to his
home.

When I walked into his apartment in New York, I
was ushered into a large room.

Mr. Dewey was lying in bed, ill, I suppose. In
this room was a young woman and two very young
children. These children were running around, playing
and having fun.

Mr. Dewey introduced them to me. "This is Mrs.
Dewey and these are my children." This young wife got
him a pen and he autographed my books.

I'll never forget the scene. Here this great old
man, happy and gentle, deep thinking; happy with the
laughter of these two adopted, young children. Here
this old wrinkled faced old man smiling and happy.
This is only for a Rembrandt to capture the spirit of
this overwhelming scene.

That's all I can tell you.

Sincerely,

Norman Unger

158

2007 E. Balboa
Temple, Az.   85281

Dear Dr. Williams:

    I saw your note in 5/24/70 N.Y. Times and am
writing to put you on the trail of a friend of John
Dewey - who knew him well.   Maybe you have his name -
but, if not, here it is.

            Dr. George E. Axtelle
            School of Education
            Int'l University   U.S.I.U.
            (formerly Cal Western)
            San Diego, Cal.

    Sorry I can't remember those new initials exactly
- but that will get him.   He lives in San Diego - and
I'm sure has a listed phone.

                        Sincerely,

                        Jeannette Veatch (Miss)

Villemain, Francis T., and Nathaniel L. Champlin,
        "Frontiers for an Experimentalist Philosophy
        of Education," <u>The Antioch Review</u>. XIX
        (Fall, 1959), 345-359.

An examination of his theory of experience and his vision of the <u>Summum Bonum</u> shows him to be a philosopher of art above all else. - 346

In the Dewey view of the nature of experience, the esthetic is so central that we cannot have an experience without it. - 346

.....the qualitative or esthetic is ever present whether the experience is primarily of a painting or of a mathematical formula. - 347

White, Morton. <u>The Age of Analysis</u>. New York:
       Mentor Books, 1955.

     .....Dewey the pragmatic philosopher of morals,
..... - 154

     But American philosophers who learned from Peirce,
James, Dewey, Royce, and Santayana became part of a
more international, cosmopolitan tradition in philosophy which was less motivated by national concern and
less burdened by xenophobia than any other group of
philosophers in the world......American philosophy in
the twentieth century has not been parochial. - 174

     .....from his [Dewey's] defense of Sacco and
Vanzetti, to his attack on the Moscow trials he was the
conscience of American philosophy. - 175

     .....Dewey, Santayana, and Whitehead - three of
the great English-speaking philosophers of the
twentieth century - have been philosophers in the grand
manner,..... - 238

Wilds, Elmer Harrison and Lottich, Kenneth V. <u>The
Foundations of Modern Education</u>. New York:
Holt, Rinehart and Winston, Inc., 1936 -
pp. 433-434.

Dewey had many disciples, among the most influential of
whom were William H. Kilpatrick, Boyd H. Bode, Thomas
H. Briggs, Ross L. Finney, and George S. Counts. These
so-called "Molders of the American mind" have not been
in complete agreement in all phases of their thinking,
but they have shared an emphasis on a social philosophy
of education.

26 Maryland Avenue
Saranac Lake, New York   12983

May 31, 1970

Mr. Robert Bruce Williams
Montclair State College
Upper Montclair, NJ

Dear Mr. Bruce:

Mr. John Dewey was the founder of the Lake Placid
Club, in Lake Placid, New York. You may be able to
get the information, from the Club, which you
require.

Best wishes,

Louise Williams
(Mrs. T. Edward Williams)

Williams, Robert Bruce. "John Dewey and Oil City,"
        Peabody Journal of Education, 46 (January,
        1969), 223-226.

Bernstein reports that Dewey "continued his reading in
philosophy" while in Oil City,[1] and Eastman recalls
that he refused to invest in Standard Oil and instead,
"borrowed books and used the oil in a lamp."[2] What
typical Deweyan practicality! Utilization of oil in a
very real sense was more appealing to him than speculative investment. This down-to-earth emphasis was
possibly nourished by the smack of the mundane that is
found in the writings of Walt Whitman. Eastman writes
that Dewey had apparently been reading Whitman's works
at this time.[3] It will be recalled that William James,
of similar philosophical persuasion, was also intrigued
by Whitman.[4]

[1]Richard J. Bernstein, _John Dewey_, p. 26.
[2]Max Eastman, _Heroes I Have Known_, p. 283.
[3]Ibid., p. 284.
[4]William James, _Pragmatism_, pp. 178-179.

American International College
Springfield, Massachusetts 01109

Dear Professor Williams:

In response to your communication of May 1st regarding items connected with John Dewey:

The enclosed is a copy of a letter I received from
John Dewey in 1939. I had been teaching in Puerto
Rico and part of my assignment had me teaching an ele-
mentary class in a one room school which carried the
name John Dewey School. I dropped Dewey a note to this
effect and he wrote back the enclosed.

This is not exactly the sort of personal reminiscence you had in mind. I saw Dewey but once. He was
speaking as a political candidate in New York City at
the Community Church. That was in 1930, and my memory
allows me no more than this. Here at American International College we were celebrating Dewey's centennial
year. One of my students whose family spent their
vacation in Nova Scotia each summer had been neighbors
of Dewey's there. They were frequent bridge partners.
Dr. Anderson (MD) the father of my student observed to
me: "One would never know from these contacts in the
summer that Dewey was one of the world's great men."
Judith Anderson brought in a picture of Dewey in swim
trunks. Those old blue kind with a white belt and a
white top shirt.

This is pretty slight and I fear nothing that you
can use. But the letter is indicative of Dewey's re-
sponsiveness.

Sincerely,

Kenneth Winetrout
Margaret C. Ells Professor of
    Education

Sept. 3rd, 1970
10 Hickory Lane
Hampden, Mass. 01036

165

```
                    John Dewey
            320 East 72nd Street
               New York City


Hubbards, Nova Scotia


                                   July 24 '39



Dear Mr. Winetrout:

     It was indeed kind of you to write me and send me
the snapshot of the school named after me in Porto
Rico - I hadn't known of it and am made quite proud as
I have more interest in some ways in such schools than
in big city mass production schools.

     I am sure you found your work in Columbus
interesting and valuable.  I have been there with Dr.
Bode's group at various times and found the atmosphere
most stimulating.

     I hope you won't allow the Logic to be too much
of a bother.

                                   Sincerely yours,



                                   (s) John Dewey
```

Bank Street College of Education
216 West Fourteenth Street
New York, NY 10011

May 26, 1970

Robert Bruce Williams
Montclair State College
Upper Montclair, New Jersey 07043

Dear Mr. Williams:

In response to your note in the "Times" on Sunday, I should like to inform you of some material which is in my possession. A very long time ago, a connection with Elsie Clapp, who as you may know worked very closely with Dr. Dewey, resulted in my receiving through her sister, a large amount of material of Dr. Dewey's work. I made a slight attempt at one time to reach the people in Carbondale who were working on a collection of Dewey's work but without success. If you are interested, I would be glad to make an appointment with you to meet with me at the College so that you may examine what we have.

Since it fills the better part of a file drawer, it would be impractical to do it any other way. As you probably know, the semester is drawing to a close but I shall be in town and available through July. If you wish to see the material, please call me at the office: CH 3-4903 - or at home: PL 2-3962.

Sincerely,

(Mrs.) Charlotte B. Winsor,
Distinguished Teacher Education
Specialist

CBW:gl

Bank Street College of Education
New York, NY

Observations on John Dewey by Dr. Charlotte B. Winsor, Distinguished Teacher Education Specialist, Bank Street College of Education, New York, NY.

June 11, 1970

My Dewey course was more or less a disaster. You sat in alphabetical order. There were 200 in the class. An assistant walked up and down and took attendance. I had to try to keep awake. My name was Biber and I was right up front. I was seventeen or eighteen then and was a senior at Teachers College, Columbia University. Dewey was not an exciting lecturer. His books - you have to read them several times.

In the early 1920's Dewey was interested in the labor movement. He was also interested in young people. He used to come down every Sunday and talk to a group of clothing cutters about his philosophy of life.....an American philosophy. At that time he looked so old to me and I was impressed with his tremendous willingness to give his time to these workers. It was an inspiring thing. Most were Jewish immigrants and he was really making a genuine attempt at communication.

At his 90th birthday party (1950), I was there. Everybody was there. The attendance was a wonderful tribute to his life. Trade union people, as well as educators and political people were present.

After the birthday cake in the presence of many "adopted children," all came to sing "Happy Birthday" to him. Then the dinner chairman announced that Mrs. Ghandi and Nehru were present. Dewey then made an impassioned plea concerning the social scene. If this society offers opportunities for moving our society forward, then we must bend all our efforts. His closing words were, "If not, not." There followed a great ovation.

RBW:eb

168

Washington University
Graduate Institute of Education
McMillan Hall
St. Louis, Missouri 63130

May 5, 1970

Dear Dr. Williams:

You might send this [letter of inquiry concerning the Dewey study] to W.W. Charters, Jr., Educational Administration, University of Oregon, Eugene,
Oregon, to send on to his mother. She was a student
at the University of Chicago in the 90's and knew
Dewey there.

Good luck.

Dr. Arthur W. Wirth

169

Wirth, Arthur G. John Dewey as Educator: His Design
    for Work in Education (1894-1904). New York:
    John Wiley & Sons, Inc., 1966. pp. 45-46-50.

    The young Dewey joined forces with the old warrio
Colonel Parker on a number of specific issues, and the
often worked from the same podium. A newspaper accoun
of one of their meetings describes the contrast of
their platform styles and also the personality of
Dewey.

    "It was my privilege recently to be present at th
last one of a series of lectures on psychology by Dr.
Dewey.....His course of lectures was delivered at the
Cook County Normal School. If one had been deaf, the
interest in watching the 'personnel' of the two famous
men, Dr. Dewey and Col. Parker, the psychologist whose
fame is not confined to his own country, would have
been enough to repay one for coming. Dr. Dewey is one
of the quietest and most modest appearing men imagina-
ble. He appears like a gentle young man who is studious and willing to learn. To see him on the platform
in his gray sack coat, drooping moustache, hair parted
in the middle and his 'excuse me for intruding' air, as
opposed to Col. Parker, with his massive bald head, his
impressive and aggressive personality and his 'you had
better not get in my way' air one would never dream
that the quiet man with his level eyebrows and pleasant
gentle voice was the lion, and the great Colonel Parker
was the lamb.

    "Such, however, is the case. Col. Parker sits at
one side of the platform, listening, often with closed
eyes, as is his wont, to the agreeable voice of Dr.
Dewey, as he quietly utters those radical ideas which
simply remove the bottom from all existing forms of
educational effort, excepting those scattered in-
stances, here and there, or those who are applying the
right methods, or those who, natural teachers, apply
them unconsciously. Col. Parker, in his aggressively
earnest way, has been lustily pounding for years, on
the same thing. Dr. Dewey does not pound. He quietly
loosens the hoops, and the bottom insensibly vanishes.

    "Dr. Dewey is worshipped by his hearers. There is
a charm about his personality which is simply irresist-
ible. He is as simple in his language as in his manner, and the ease with which even the great unwashed
can comprehend the principles he lays down is proof of
his grandeur.

"At the close of the lecture--which in itself is artistic, for instead of sending off a literary sky-rocket at the end, he simply turns away from the board and melts into the nearest chair--one of the bright girls of the training-class stepped up and handed him a beautiful bouquet of pink and white carnations.....

"He rose, and true to his nature, uttered just the right thing, in about six words, thanking his listeners for the stimulus they had furnished him, which was all a man could desire.

"Col. Parker then arose, and in an unnaturally tame voice, which indicated to those who know him best a mighty surging torrent of emotion within, said: 'Ladies and gentlemen, if what Dr. Dewey has been telling you is true, the millions upon millions which are expended upon our public school system is not only spent in the wrong way, but we are dulling bright intellects and doing incalculable harm to the future generations.....'"[1]

He often could be seen in lively, informal discussion with one or more colleagues from his own or other departments.[2] Many of the leading scholars and departmental chairmen were genuinely interested in educational problems of the lower school. One could see evidence of their influence and participation in many of the features of the Laboratory School.[3]

---

[1]George Dykhuizen, "John Dewey: The Chicago Years," Journal of the History of Philosophy, Vol. 2, No. 2 (October, 1964), pp. 246-247, quoting from Ellen Eames DeGraff, "Chicago Happenings. Of Interest to Evans-villians--Something about Psychology." This is a newspaper account appearing in a Chicago or Evansville paper sometime in late 1894. The clipping is to be found in Colonel Parker's Scrapbook, University Archives.
[2]Reported in conversations with Dr. (Mrs.) W.W. Charters and Dr. Frederick Eby, who were graduate students in the department at the same time.
[3]Katherine C. Mayhew and Anna C. Edwards, The Dewey School (New York, Appleton-Century-Crofts, 1936), pp. 4 and 10.

George A. Wolf Jr. M.D.
Jericho Center
Vermont 05465

6/6/70

Dear Professor Williams,

     The story I promised is as follows. In 1947 or 8
I was a young physician practicing medicine in New York
City. One week end a professor of mine who was Dr.
Dewey's physician had to leave town and asked me to
take his emergency calls. Dr. Dewey had gone for a
walk on 5th ave. slipped and hurt his shoulder. I was
called to see him which I did in his apartment. The
old gentlemen was literally quivering in pain and his
new wife was most apprehensive. Normally one would
handle such a problem in N.Y.C. by either calling an
orthopedic physician or sending the patient to the hospital for possible reduction by an orthopedist under
anesthesia. I am an internist but I remembered from
medical school orthopedics a maneuver, somewhat old
fashioned, said to reduce such dislocations occasionally.

     The patient was in so much pain that I decided to
try the maneuver. It consisted of taking off my shoe,
sitting on the foot of Dr. Dewey's bed, placing my sock
covered foot in Dr. Dewey's armpit, grasping his hand
and forearm on the affected side and gently pulling. I
had some trepidation because I had remembered that
pulling hard in such cases might injure the brachial
plexus. I was thus very gentle but apprehensive lest I
do harm. His muscles were not strong so pulling did
not add to his pain. Suddenly, there was a feeling
that the bone had slipped back into place. My memory
tells me that it was a loud satisfying crack but my
biological training tells me that both Dr. Dewey and I
were so relieved, he of his pain and I of my apprehen-
sion, that the event was really very quiet. He stopped
shaking looked at me gratefully and smiled a little
smile. He said the appropriate thank yous as did his
wife.

172

The amusing part was that as I put my foot in the suffering gentleman's armpit (axilla), I said "Pardon me, Dr. Dewey."

As an aside, 1 year later I bought a summer home in Vermont and in 1952 I moved to Burlington, Vermont.

Sincerely,

Geo. A. Wolf, Jr.

Dear Dr. Wolff:

Thank you for the xerox copies of your correspondence
with Professor Dewey. I was especially intrigued by
Dewey's treatment of the word, "phenomenological." He
constantly emphasizes the practical aspects, and often
shys away from the purely abstract if its application
to an immediate problem seems remote.

My main interest, of course, has to do with the individuals' personal recollections of Dewey. The correspondence you so kindly sent me is warmly appreciated.
If, however, you can jot down a few sentences, it would
be very helpful. For example, your most vivid recollection of Dewey; how you look upon him as a person, a
philosopher; how you place him as a philosopher; or a
personal anecdote. These are mere suggestions. Any
one of them, if treated by you, would be most helpful.

Again ... sincere thanks for the correspondence.

                              Sincerely yours,

                              Robert Bruce Williams, Ed.D.
                              Associate Professor of
                              Education and Social Work

RBW:oxy

Dr. Kurt H. Wolff
Brandeis University
Waltham, Massachusetts 02154

June 8, 1 9 7 0

174

BRANDEIS UNIVERSITY
Waltham, Massachusetts 02154

Department of Sociology

14.ix.70

Dear Professor Williams,

Thank you for your friendly note of 8.vi. I found it
only now, on returning from Europe. I am sorry that I
can't be of any help to you inasmuch as I never met
John Dewey. The correspondence started by his sending
me, as far as I recall, a reprint of a paper of his,
and this on the basis of something I had published and
- I think - sent him a reprint of. Please keep me
posted on the progress of your work.

With best regards and wishes.

Sincerely yours,

Kurt H. Wolff

MONTCLAIR STATE COLLEGE
Upper Montclair, New Jersey 07043

May 10, 1971

Dr. Kurt H. Wolff
Department of Sociology
Brandeis University
Waltham, Mass. 02154

Dear Dr. Wolff:

I continue to feel very grateful to you for your cooperation concerning my research on John Dewey reminiscences. I am interested in photo-copying the brief
letter to you from Mr. Dewey under date of September
30, 1948 in which he makes the interesting comment, "I
believe the future of philosophy is closely bound up
with developments in sociological science," since the
latter has to get down to "brass tacks" more than the
physical sciences. Sincerely yours, John Dewey." I do
not plan to interpret or elaborate upon the letter. Is
this satisfactory with you?

I also am intrigued by a brief statement in his letter
to you of November 2, 1948 in which he writes, "I can't
think of anything which I should find more interesting
than your material on the sociology of knowledge; as I
wrote before my knowledge of the literature is limited
to Mannheim. I shall be happy to receive your mimeographed material. To try to make acquaintance first
hand would be beyond my powers and I have felt my ignorance a handicap for a long time." In this same letter
he points out that the business of the philosopher "is
to help develop a method for systematically carrying on
valuation of the subjectmatters the sociologist reports. This is perhaps a clearer tho condensed statement of the kind of cooperation between sociology and
philosophy that seems to me important."

Later that same month, November 12, 1948, he elaborates
the theme, "I am inclined to think that if it were
clearly seen that sociological facts bear the same
intimate relation to formation of policies of social
action (including what is properly moral in value) that

176

physical science bears to recognized formation of policies in physical engineering, the work of sociologists
would be much more effective than it is now . . . It
seems to me that a good many persons today who are
called sociologists 'don't' have any very clear idea of
what they are about or what their subjectmatter is.
Theory and fact are two aspects of one and the same
transaction."

If I should decide to use other excerpts from the correspondence, would you care to know in advance? In the
meantime, the excerpts that I have quoted to you are
the only ones that I am now planning to use.

Sincerely yours,

Robert Bruce Williams
Associate Professor of Education
and Social Work

RBW:eb

YORK UNIVERSITY
Faculty of Arts & Sciences
4700 Keele Street
Downsview 463, Ontario

Department of Sociology

20.v.71

Dear Professor Williams,

Thank you for your letter of the 10th just received,
forwarded from Brandeis. (I have been a visiting
professor here this past semester and can be reached
at this address until June 10, after which it is
Brandeis again.)

I am glad you found some passages in John Dewey's
letters to me usable and approve of your using the
ones you quote in your letter. Yes, I'd appreciate
knowing in advance what others, if any, you might
want to use in addition. I take it that you'll
indicate source and date.

Sincerely yours,

Kurt H. Wolff

1158 Fifth Avenue
New York 29, New York

September 30, 1948

Dear Dr. Wolff,

    Thanks for letter and reprint. I have not read
them yet as they only just arrived.....[They] moved me
to send you a copy of my Journal article.   I want to
say now that I believe the future of philosophy is
closely bound up with developments in sociological
science, since the latter has to get down to "brass
tacks" more than the physical sciences.

                              Sincerely yours,

                              John Dewey

1158 Fifth Avenue
New York 29, New York

November 2, 1948

Dear Kurt Wolff:

.....I can't think of anything which I should find
more interesting than your material on the sociology
of knowledge; as I wrote before, my knowledge of the
literature is limited to Mannheim. I shall be happy
to receive your mimeographed material. To try to
make acquaintance at firsthand would be beyond my
powers and I have felt my ignorance a handicap for a
long time.....[The business of the philosopher] is to
help develop a method for systematically carrying on
valuation of the subjectmatters, the sociologist
reports. This is perhaps a clearer though condensed
statement of the kind of cooperation between
sociology and philosophy that seems to me important.

                              Sincerely yours,

                              John Dewey

1158 Fifth Avenue
New York 29, New York

November 12, 1948

Dear Dr. Wolff:

.....I am inclined to think that if it were clearly
seen that sociological facts bear the same intimate
relation to formation of policies of social action
(including what is properly moral in value) that
physical science bears to recognized formation of
policies in physical engineering, the work of
sociologists would be much more effective than it is
now.....It seems to me that a good many persons today
who are called sociologists don't have any very clear
idea of what they are about or what their subjectmatter is. Theory and fact are two aspects of one
and the same transaction.

Sincerely yours,

John Dewey

ABOUT THE AUTHOR

Robert Bruce Williams is a native of Oil City, Pennsylvania, whose high school once listed John Dewey as one of its teachers (see "John Dewey and Oil City," p.164). Dr. Williams received the A.B. degree from Occidental College. Both the masters and doctorate were awarded by Rutgers University. The major focus was on social and philosophical foundations of education. He also studied at Carnegie-Mellon University, University of Pittsburgh, and Columbia University. He has been associated with Montclair State College for fourteen years. As graduate professor, he has taught such courses as Philosophy of Education, Medical Problems in Education, Counseling Techniques, and School Social Work (Social Casework). He has also taught at Fairleigh Dickinson University, Trenton State College, and Wayne State University.

Dr. Williams' wide range of interests is reflected in publications that have appeared in a variety of fields, such as social work, medicine, psychology of music (published in USA and abroad), sociology (developed the "role analysis paradigm"), history, hymnology, industrial arts education, poetry (authored the fifth stanza of "America"), school health and philosophy. In addition to the present volume, he co-authored The Educator Faces Social Issues (Montclair State College, 1970), and School Vandalism: Cause and Cure (Century 21 Press, 1981).

He has held memberships in the Philosophy of Education Society, the John Dewey Society, the American Association of University Professors, National Association of Social Workers, International Association of Pupil Personnel Workers, and Phi Delta Kappa. He is listed in Who's Who in the East, the Dictionary of International Biography, Directory of American Philosophers, Notable Americans, and Leaders in Education. He resides with his wife, Ruth, and younger son, David, in Roseland, New Jersey.

182

INDEX

A

	Page
Absent-minded	86
A Common Faith	38
Adams, George P.	1
Addams, Jane	29, 69, 114, 118
Ames, Adelbert	79
Adopted children	168
Alexander Technique	79
Alport, Gordon	2
Altman, Jules	131
American Civil Liberties Union	54
American Federation of Teachers	62
American genius	35
American Humanist Association	152
American Philosophical Association	57
Ames-Cantril	88
Antifascist and anticommunist	54
Antioch Review	160
April Fool's Day	37
Archambault, Reginald D.	3
Art as Experience	45
Artificial problems	149
Art in Painting, The	125
Arts	8, 9
Autobiography of Bertrand Russell, The	136
Ayers, Clarence E.	115
Axtelle, George E.	4, 5, 159

B

Bacons, The	76
Bahm, Archie	7
Bangkok (College of Education)	11
Barnes, Albert C.	45, 53, 114, 132
Barnes Foundation	8, 45, 125
Bashful	37
Beatty	141
Bentley, Arthur F.	131
Bernstein, Richard J.	10, 44
Birthday party	28
Blew up a test tube	105
Bode, Boyd	22, 29, 95, 121
Borroman, Merle L.	13
Bosanquet	76

183

O

P

T